E. Dobiášová, Š. Sekaninová & J. Sedláčková

ATLAS OF DOGS

Illustrations by Marcel Králik

Albatros

This book belongs
to all dog lovers!

TABLE OF CONTENTS

iNTRODUCTiON

It is said that dogs are human's best friends. And we can agree with that. Paintings in prehistoric caves around the world show that we have been living, doing sports, helping, and working by their sides for thousands, perhaps tens of thousands of years. We've learned a lot during that time, such as:

... how to fetch

... and especially how to leave a scent mark behind for all of our fellow dogs anytime and anywhere (you know, we are able to learn a great deal of information from it—for example, which dog went by, whether it was a male or a female, how old it was, or even its mood).

... how to shake!

... how to save the best treats for later (what if someone else eats them?!)

In addition, we know how to make those puppy--dog eyes so you sometimes forgive us when we get into trouble.

When you leave the house, we are sad, but when you return, we are filled with joy and immediately welcome you at the door! Sometimes, we even jump on your shoulders and lick you from head to toe ... That's just the way we are!

WE ARE ALSO ANIMALS WITH PERFECTLY DEVELOPED SENSES . . . YOU DON'T BELIEVE US?

🐾 We have about 20 times more scent receptor cells than humans. The moist surface of our nose catches every scent.

🐾 We cool down our body by sticking out our long tongue. You should try it too!

🐾 We can learn to understand up to 165 human words.

🐾 It is said that we, dogs, are color-blind. But that's not true at all! However, the palette of colors we can see is limited compared with humans; it is also less vibrant.

🐾 Woof woof! We have 42 sharp teeth!

🐾 Can you hear the storm in the distance? No? Well, due to our great hearing, we can! We also use ear movements for communication.

🐾 When we're happy, we wag our tail!

🐾 We may move our paws when we're asleep. This happens when we dream about running somewhere.

🐾 We only produce sweat on our paws!

🐾 Did you know that we, dogs, poop in alignment with the Earth's magnetic field?

Let's take a closer look at the strangest and most interesting dog breeds and read stories from their daily lives!

DESCENDANTS OF WILD WOLVES

Just imagine that all the dogs in the world, even the smallest and cutest chihuahuas, are descendants of wild wolves that inhabited the dense forests and vast steppes in the harshest corners of the world!

DOG TO HUMAN YEARS CONVERTER

Dog size	Small: under 20 lbs	Medium: 20-50 lbs	Large: over 50 lbs
Dog years	Human years		
1	15	15	15
2	24	24	24
3	28	28	28
5	36	36	36
10	56	60	66
15	76	83	93

SIGHTHOUNDS

These long-legged, handsome dogs are aristocratic. They always think twice before they give you their paw, or they might just as well ignore you. They can be loyal companions to their owners. Although they might be a little bit stubborn at times, they enjoy going out on a walk, running next to your bike, or proudly participating in a greyhound sprint race.

INTELLIGENCE: 🐾🐾🐾🐾🐾
OBEDIENCE: 🐾🐾🐾
ACTIVITY: Racing dogs
GUARDING: 🐾 (You'd better lock the door!)
BARKING: We rarely bark ...
FAMILY TYPE: Aristodogs (We are quiet and well mannered.)
IDEAL HOME: House with a garden

IRISH WOLFHOUND ➤➤

Don't panic, my friends! Despite my scary appearance, I'm really a kind and friendly dog. I'm even nice to strangers and visitors, and I hardly ever bark at them. I would love an owner with a large garden, where I can run around whenever I feel like it.

⬅ RUSSIAN WOLFHOUND

I used to adorn Russian palaces. The aristocracy often took me with them when they went hunting in the fall. To this day, I have kept those graceful movements of jumping in the woods over trunks of trees and over streams. Although I require gentle treatment, I will reward you with the same amount of tenderness and peace.

GREYHOUND PARK

8

4

↑ ENGLISH GREYHOUND

I used to be a hunting dog, but nowadays, I'm more into dog racing. I can run at speeds of up to 37.3 miles per hour during sprints. I like the warmth of a family fireplace, and although I might not seem like it, I will even move into a flat with you.

AFGHAN HOUND ➡

My pedigree is full of dog aristocracy and runs deep into the past. I need an experienced owner who can train me despite my slightly free-minded and stubborn character and who will regularly comb my beautiful silky soft coat.

OTHERS OF THE GREYHOUND FAMILY

1. ARABIAN GREYHOUND (SLOUGHI): I am a sensitive gentleman, whose mind is a little bit complicated. I don't trust just anybody. And sometimes I like to chase other pets ...

2. PERSIAN GREYHOUND (SALUKI): At home, I'm as gentle as a lamb, but outside, you better hold the lead firmly!

3. WHIPPET: When it gets cold outside in the winter, give me a warm coat so that I don't get sick. That applies to all of us, shorthair hounds!

4. AZAVAK: I come from hot Africa. When it's cold outside, there is no way I'm leaving my bed.

5. DEERHOUND: Thanks to my longer coat, I don't mind going for a walk even in the fall, when it's foggy and rainy.

← ITALIAN GREYHOUND

I am an obedient and gentle dog with a lively character. If you don't want your dog to be as big as you or even bigger, I am your type. As a little greyhound, my legs are shorter than those of my relatives, but I am just as elegant and noble!

DOGS' POST

Daily

316th YEAR — VOLUME 4 🐾 No. 3789 🐾 SATURDAY, APRIL 14, 1928 🐾 35 DOG HAIRS

MICK THE MILLER, THE CHAMPION

LADIES AND GENTLEMAN, ATHLETES AND GREYHOUNDS, PAW ON YOUR HEART, WHO WOULD LIKE TO ACHIEVE THE SAME SUCCESS AS THE MOST FAMOUS GREYHOUND RECORD HOLDER AND PROMOTER OF GREYHOUND RACING, MICK THE MILLER? HOW CAN YOU DO SO? READ AN INSPIRATIVE INTERVIEW.

Mr. Mick, how did you get into running?
Look, young man, I was born in 1926 in the house of an Irish parish curator in the village of Killeigh. You would naturally expect me to study rather than do sports. But you know how it is. At that time, a certain Michael Green was working on the parsonage. He saw a promising athlete in me, even though I was just a puppy with milk on my whiskers. Well, he took me in and worked his magic!

What do you mean by that?
Every day, I had to train and work hard under his supervision. A lot of blood, sweat, and tears went into it, but I soon began to enjoy it, especially when the results came. I won 15 out of 20 races.

How did your career progress?
How?! I made it to all the prestigious English derby races, and I broke the world record by running 1,575 ft in under 30 seconds. I took part in 48 races and won 36 of them decisively. Not a bad score, wouldn't you say, Mr. Journalist? (Mick The Miller barked happily, ed.)

Mr. Miller, you made greyhound racing popular thanks to your achievements, didn't you?
Yeah, yeah, that's what they say. I participated in more races year by year, and people cheered for me. They were crazy about me like I was some kind of celebrity, but I wasn't. I was just an enthusiastic athlete with a little talent.

Mick The Miller is such a humble greyhound. The truth is that if it weren't for him, greyhound races might not even be taking place now. Their existence was truly threatened.

SCENT HOUNDS

Arf-arf! As soon as our mighty bark echoes through the woods, animals run and hide. We're masters at tracking, and every hunter thinks highly of us. We're independent while hunting and also stand our ground during our upbringing. Go shake paws with somebody else; we have our dignity. We come to love family life, but as soon as we pick up a scent while we're out on a walk, we're gone with the wind. See you in a bit!

INTELLIGENCE: 🐾🐾🐾🐾🐾

OBEDIENCE: 🐾🐾🐾

ACTIVITY: Hunters

GUARDING: 🐾🐾🐾

BARKING: You can recognize all sorts of things just by the tone of our voice.

FAMILY TYPE: Over the centuries, we have become friendly companions.

IDEAL HOME: Watch out for furniture and flower beds!

LARGE SCENT HOUNDS

BLUE GASCONY BASSET ➡️

Woof, woof! Can you hear my beautiful baritone? I'll charm more than one female heart with my deep voice as well as my warm nature. Rabbits are not all that happy to see me though. I don't know a better feeling than when I give them a good chase with friends from my pack. Well, I'm a hunter, no point in denying that.

⬅️ OTTERHOUND

What I'm about to tell you is going to blow your mind. Ready? I have webbed feet. Really, I'm not lying! I hope it won't make you sad, but I can swim faster than you. I'm a pro at diving too. Otters would tell you. People used me for hunting otters for several centuries, but those days are gone. Nowadays, I'm a rather good companion and a good guard dog. I don't jump into anything except for water. I think everything through before I act.

← ENGLISH AND AMERICAN FOXHOUNDS

Woof, woof, woof! Don't take it personally, but our best friend needs to have fur, four paws, and a tail. What's that? Are we talking about foxes? Growl, we can't stand them, but when they happen to come across our path, we'll catch them in no time! Naturally, we have a dog in mind. For centuries, we've been living in packs and we do best alongside our own species. We can even keep up with horses with our long athletic legs! The American foxhound can confirm this with its melodic and long howl—that's how it expresses joy. But you don't want to hear it while hunting! Foxes, run for your lives!

ENGLISH FOXHOUND

AMERICAN FOXHOUND

BLOODHOUND →

I am undoubtedly the king among bloodhounds. My sense of smell is up to 40 times more sensitive than yours. I can even sniff a scent that's up to two weeks old. Hunters, as well as policemen and paramedics, worship us almost as gods. It's really easy for me to find the culprit, someone missing, or an injured person. I probably look like I munch on onions often or like I'm about to start crying, but don't be fooled—that's not the case! I love to cuddle and every caress of yours is as welcome to me as a juicy piece of steak. I'll have one more, please!

← BLACK AND TAN COONHOUND

Raccoons, you better watch out! They think they are clean, but I can detect their scent even with a stuffy nose. Then, I'll corner them up in a tree and call triumphantly for my master. That's my job. Just like all hunting dogs, I also have a mind of my own and can be quite stubborn. That's why I need a confident and equally stubborn and clever master, who will set clear boundaries for me.

DOGS' POST

DAILY

1st YEAR — VOLUME 1 🐾 No. 1 🐾 FRIDAY, JULY 26, 1613 🐾 35 DOG HAIRS

DONNCHADH, THE HOUND WHO SAVED THE KING OF SCOTLAND

A Window into History

Four-legged furry and less furry representatives of the dog world have impacted both ancient and recent history. You don't believe me? Think of bloodhound Donnchadh, a loyal dog who saved the future King of Scotland.

Donnchadh (pronounced don-nu-chu) was a companion of Robert the Bruce, a valiant warrior who fought for the independence of Scotland in the fourteenth century. As is common among power-hungry people, this initiative wasn't appreciated by Edward I, who wanted the whole Scotland for himself. He ordered his henchmen and supporters to capture Robert and all his companions.

And his orders were carried out. Edward's patrol burst into Robert's house, but they only found his wife and dog Donnchadh. "We have Donnchadh! He will lead us to his master," rejoiced the English soldiers. And they were right. Loyal Donnchadh followed Robert, who was in hiding, and revealed, his master's hideaway by mistake. It seemed as if the history of Scotland would lose its hero when Donnchadh unexpectedly attacked the enemies! He saved his beloved master and the future King of Scotland.

POLISH HOUND (OGAR POLSKI) ➔

Once upon a time there was a Polish Hound who got lost in the woods . . . ha ha ha, good one! We, Ogars, don't get lost in the woods that easily. We have great orientation skills and a sensitive sense of smell. Don't worry about us when we run away—we might have a mind of our own, but we'd recognize your scent among thousands of others. Once you hear our mighty voice, come look at what we found: a wild boar! It might get a bit difficult, however, with the whole "fetch" thing . . .

MIDDLE-SIZED SCENT HOUNDS

← DUNKER (NORWEGIAN HOUND)

When I walk down the street, all the eyes of female dogs are on me. I am colorful like no other dog. But rather than female dogs, I like to chase animals—I go crazy when I smell hares and foxes; let me at them! That's how it is with us, hunters. Loneliness doesn't bother me, which is why you can leave me outdoors all year round. But if you don't keep me sufficiently occupied, then beware of your tulip beds. Tug and pluck!

TRANSYLVANIAN HOUND ➔

Cats, you better watch out! I'm a hunter from the tip of my sensitive nose to the last hair on my tail. I like to make my own decisions, which has benefited me multiple times while hunting. I'm intelligent and bright, but don't try doing the "high five" command with me. My upbringing might make it tough for families with kids, but hunters will know how to handle me.

OTHER BREEDS OF THE SCENT HOUND FAMILY

1. SPANISH SCENTHOUND: I don't know if it's true, but apparently, I am descended from ancient Celtic hunting dogs. And when you stretch out my ears, they can reach the tip of my nose.

2. BERNER NIEDERLAUFHUND: The thing I love the most is to run through the woods. I don't fit in cities and I'm not suitable for lazy owners. So don't sit with your nose in a book: let's go for a run!

3. LUZERNER NIEDERLAUFHUND: I come from the Swiss city of Lucerne, and I am fine with hunting all by myself. I won't say no, however, to a pack, whether it's a dog one or yours!

4. FAWN BRITTANY GRIFFON: Attention, please, I spot some wildlife: woof woof woof! No terrain is an obstacle for me, and I won't get lost either.

5. FINNISH HOUND: You shouldn't rely too much on me with guarding your home, but I will make sure to tell you about every prey that I catch.

PORCELAIN ➡

I am a born aristocrat with my noble appearance and posh manners. But I'm definitely no fragile porcelain doll. My passion is to hunt, preferably in a pack, and I definitely don't lack courage. I am happy when I manage to catch a hare, doe, or a wild boar.

BAVARIAN AND HANOVER HOUNDS ➡

Can you smell it too? I mean the distinct smell of clover in the coat of a hare that is hopping over the hill. No? Follow me then! We've been living alongside hunters since long ago, and our great sense of smell is legendary. We are born trackers. The Hanover Hound gets along with children but I, the Bavarian Hound, woof woof, can't seem to understand them!

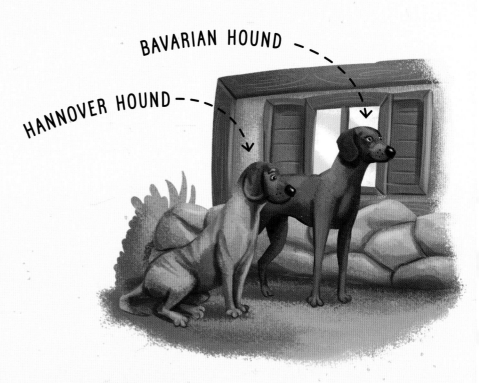

BAVARIAN HOUND - - - >

HANNOVER HOUND - - - >

SMALL SCENT HOUNDS

⬅ BEAGLE

I belong to an ancient breed. My family tree goes all the way back to the fifteenth century. I used to hunt trouble-makers like jackals in Sudan or wild boars in Sri Lanka: those were the days! I like to roam around in my free time. As soon as I catch a scent, you won't be able to stop me in time: farewell—you'll see me in a couple of hours. As you can see, I don't exactly rank among the most obedient breeds, but my adorable face will make you forgive all of my mischiefs, even the incessant barking.

BASSET HOUND ➡

Ouch, I stepped on my ears again! Oh well, I'm famous because of them. It's thanks to them that I am a great tracker—they swirl up the odors from the ground, which I have within reach thanks to my short legs. My owner should be tolerant, patient enough, and with a sense of humor because I like to "talk back." If you want me to drop that stick, you have to command the exact opposite—not to drop it. So there's that. And one more fun fact about my humble chubby self: given the opportunity, I like to overeat . . .

ALPINE DACHSBRACKE ➡

If I have the chance to run away, I'll do it ... Whoosh! And I'm gone. It's not that I'm disobedient, but every Alpine Dachsbracke knows that freedom smells the best, and we have a nose for it. Even hunters sing odes to our ingenious sense of smell, fearlessness, and bravery. On the other hand, we tend to have a possessive tendency and that applies especially to our family—we pamper them and shower them with kindness and loyalty.

— EVEN IF IT'S COLD, I AM HAPPY!

RELATED BREEDS

⬅ DALMATIAN

Everybody knows us, Dalmatians: slender dogs with whimsical black and white spots. But few may know that back in the eighteenth century, we used to trot alongside the royal coaches of noblemen. We used to be their guides, guardians, and even bodyguards as they made their way through waving crowds. Do you like running or other sports? Then we're yours. We're persistent, friendly, and curious. What are you saying? I can't hear you! You know, sometimes we are a bit deaf.

RHODESIAN RIDGEBACK ➡

My grandfathers used to tell me stories about how they used to guard their masters' property in Zimbabwe, Southern Africa. They had to defend it from furious lions. They would often even start a fight with them. And when they were hungry, the whole pack could hunt down an antelope or a gazelle. I think I get my strength and courage from them. And I'll bet you anything that with the proper upbringing of an experienced master, I could become a dog warrior just like my grandfather. Now, where can I get a hold of some lions?

DOGS' POST

DAILY

394th YEAR — VOLUME 6 🐾 No. 4715 🐾 WEDNESDAY, JUNE 21, 2006 🐾 35 DOG HAIRS

Can dogs   make phone calls?

THE AMAZING BEAGLE BELLE!

READERS OF OUR DOGS' POST DAILY KNOW THAT WE, DOGS, ARE VERY INTELLIGENT. OUR HUMAN BIPED FRIENDS, HOWEVER, OFTEN UNDERESTIMATE US. FOR EXAMPLE, THEY THINK THAT WE CANNOT MAKE PHONE CALLS. WE ASKED BEAGLE BELLE TO SHARE HER OPINION WITH US.

Belle, what do you think? Are we, dogs, really unable to make phone calls?
BELLE: Nonsense, if we want to, we can do anything. Look at me, for instance—woof! (barks happily)

Have you ever made a phone call?
BELLE: Yeah, back when my master's life was at stake. He has diabetes. That day, he collapsed and I had to call for help.

How?
BELLE: Simply. I grabbed his phone with my teeth and dialed the ambulance service. I know their number by heart: 911.

You most likely saved your master's life.
BELLE: Right, but who wouldn't help their best friend?

Belle, how many phone numbers do you remember?
BELLE: I'll be honest. I only remember one number, and that's nine. The ambulance service is saved under it. My master trained me for emergency situations. If I hadn't been trained, I would have probably been lost. Making phone calls is not natural for dogs, you know? Woof, woof! I am now attending a special course to perfect my sense of smell to know in advance when my master's blood sugar is decreasing. Really! It can be predicted based on scent changes. He will never collapse again, and I'll gladly forget the number nine!

101 DALMATIANS
A story full of love, suspense, and dogs!

FROM FRIDAY AT YOUR CINEMA!

A dog is a very useful creature for its masters. It makes them go out and get some fresh air, makes them laugh, and teaches them responsibility and love. It can also help them find their one and only life partner.

Just watch the big dog hit 101 Dalmatians! The story will take you to the homes of two very different Londoners—a young man, Roger, who creates computer games, and Anita, who works as a fashion designer in a luxurious fashion boutique owned by the evil Cruella De Vil. They do have something in common, however: they each have a Dalmatian. Roger has a boy named Pongo and Anita's girl is called Perdita.

When the two of them take their dear ones out for a walk, Pongo and Perdita meet and start to fall for each other—it's dog love at first sight! And because they exchange long amorous looks all the time, they get Anita and Roger to meet as well. Before another year has come and gone, Perdita has fifteen puppies and Anita is expecting her first baby.

Their life would have been like a fairy-tale were it not for the nasty Cruella de Vil, who had an itch for the finest chic coat with Dalmatian spots, made of those little puppies! How will this end? Can Pongo, Perdita, and their human masters protect the little cuties?

The film will be shown at Bark Star Cinema.

Admission is free for puppies!

POINTERS
AND SETTERS

We are made for activity and hunting. Many hunters have been charmed by our endurance, beauty, strength, and elegance. We love to roam the woods, fields, and waters by their side. However, even if you have no interest in hunting, don't despair. Give us enough physical activity and our loyal dog hearts will belong to you in a heartbeat! We can do sports together or take looong walks through the countryside . . .

INTELLIGENCE: 🐾🐾🐾🐾🐾
OBEDIENCE: 🐾🐾🐾🐾🐾
ACTIVITY: Hunters
GUARDING: 🐾🐾

BARKING: Some of us announce capturing an animal, while others bark at every passerby.

FAMILY TYPE: We appreciate the company of a hunter.

IDEAL HOME: In the middle of woods, water, and hillsides

POINTERS—THE BRAQUE TYPE

WEIMARANER (SHORTHAIRED) ➤

There are few who would willingly admit that they have been outsmarted by a dog. When it comes to me though, that thought will probably fly through your head from time to time. Intelligence is my strong suit; unfortunately, I can be extremely stubborn. Therefore, I need a strong-willed owner so I can catch them something for dinner. I am loyal to my family, but I'd rather avoid the city.

← PUDELPOINTER

I am a composed hunter with strong nerves. I'm not scared of gunshots, and not even a mouse can evade my sensitive nose. That's why I have many admirers among huntsmen. Whenever I smell prey, I'll bend my front paw, extend my tail outward and won't move a muscle . . . But if you're not a fan of hunting, I'd very much like to jog with you! The fields, woods, and water are my second homes.

OLD DANISH POINTER AND AUVERGNE POINTING DOG ➜

We have been reputable hunters for centuries—the court of the French King Louis XIV, known as the Sun King, can attest to that. We accompanied him on hunts and never missed a single one. We love to live in a pack with others because that's what we're used to, woof woof! We are kind, friendly, and intelligent. But be warned—we tend to feel provoked by the presence of another pet, be it a cat or a canary.

AUVERGNE POINTING DOG

OLD DANISH POINTER

← VIZSLA

For more than a thousand years, I've been helping nomadic Hungarians with tracking capercaillies, pheasants, ducks, and other birds. When hunting, I am vigilant and quiet, although at home, I tend to be very talkative. I tell my suspenseful tales with barking, whining, and grumbling, and you can answer me with your own strange sounds ... I will not let you out of my sight and will watch you like a hawk. I get along best with older kids that have the same passion for adventure as I do.

SHORTHAIRED AND WIREHAIRED GERMAN POINTER ➜

My fur stings like little wires and is flat and thick, hence the name wirehaired. It protects me from the whims of the weather. And you don't have to worry about me getting cuts from thorns or branches, all thanks to my coat. Me and my shorthaired friend face everything with courage and vigilance. When it comes to hunting though, we like to decide for ourselves and may be a bit stubborn ...

SHORTHAIRED POINTER

WIREHAIRED POINTER

POINTERS—THE SPANIEL TYPE

BRITTANY (LONGHAIRED) ➜

Despite being a hunter through and through, I get on well with other animals, except for birds. Just take a look at that flock that flew off into the air the moment they spotted me! A bird will always be prey to me. That's why you need to keep your parakeet somewhere else, be it the basement, the attic … in short, nowhere near me. Don't worry, I am exceptionally cuddly and attentive when it comes to himans. I need a lot of physical activity, as all hounds do.

LARGE …

… AND SMALL

← LARGE AND SMALL MUNSTERLANDERS

We have huntsmen wrapped around our little paws. We are friendly, hard-working, and universal hunters that do not seek out conflict. Plus, we look really elegant, with soft fur and a playful facial expression … No wonder you love us as family companions. Do you want to make us happy? Throw us a ball or a branch, and we'll go fetch it, even into water! We swim well and willingly.

PICARDY SPANIEL (LONGHAIRED) ➜

Hunting in water is my specialty—woodcocks and ducks should probably pick a different pond than the one I am planning to swim in! I'll go through every river, stream, and puddle. Even Louis XII praised my hunting abilities back in the fifteenth century. Huntsmen admire my vigilance, but also my poise and composure, and they are the ones who can keep me properly occupied. But due to my gentle and friendly nature, I can be satisfied with normal company, maybe even children.

STABYHOUN ➡

C'mon, throw it already! I could play fetch for hours, days, weeks, and even years and centuries. I am full of energy, and if you don't want to go hunting with me, you'll need to keep me occupied with something else. I get on well with other dogs, and I even like children. However, my fur needs constant attention, so always keep a brush nearby.

POINTERS—THE GRIFFON TYPE

⬅ ITALIAN WIREHAIRED POINTING DOG

Do I look serious to you? That's probably due to my manicured moustache and wise expression. In reality though, I am a very happy and playful dog. Now, I'll count to three and you run and hide. With my hunter's talent, I'll be able to find you in no time! One, two, three! And I will lick you to death, woof! Human contact is as important to me as sufficient physical activity and, by the way, I drool a lot when doing both ... Yes, that puddle is my saliva.

OTHER POINTERS

1. BOURBONNAIS POINTER: You set the rules, so I swear I will not eat your canary for dinner.

2. BRACCO ITALIANO: I love being on the ground, in the water, even in the air if I could ... But do teach me how to come back on command: otherwise, I will run after everything that runs or rides!

3. FRENCH WIREHAIRED KORTHALS GRIFFON: I need an owner who will go on a walk with me, of course! The only thing is that someone will have to watch our yard while we're gone ...

4. BOHEMIAN WIREHAIRED POINTING GRIFFON: I'm an old friend of the King and Emperor, Charles IV. They say he wore a beard similar to mine.

SETTERS

POINTER ➥

When I was little and people would ask me what I wanted to become, I would bark immediately: a hunter! It's in my blood, and I use an old but proven method of hunting. As soon as I sense my prey, I stand motionless and point toward it with my nose. This is called a "pointing stance."

ENGLISH SETTER

GORDON SETTER

⬅ ENGLISH AND GORDON SETTERS

Many dog moms can attest to the fact that we are elegant and attractive. A simple touch of our soft fur, a look into our dreamy, beautiful eyes, and you're lost ... We are exceptionally cuddly, playful, and gentle. Only birds might disagree. Truth be told, we are hunters, and we will stay that way. We love swimming and long walks in the countryside. The Gordon Setter also loves new territories—let him run around! He will come back to you.

IRISH SETTER AND IRISH RED AND WHITE SETTER ➥

Thanks to our lovely, shiny fur and noble features, we have the reputation of being two of the most beautiful dog breeds. Our owner's equipment should always include a brush and a pair of walking boots. If we cannot hunt, we want to run, jump, swim, and do all sorts of other sports. Roaming the countryside full of new scents is our paradise. We will sniff out a fox in its den, a hare in the field, and even the carefully hidden food in your backpack. Yum!

IRISH SETTER

IRISH RED AND WHITE SETTER

TERRIERS

Although we may not look like it, we have the hearts of hunters and warriors. Just a flash of movement and we strike our prey. We are tough, intelligent, and head-strong. Without consistent training, we might plan to take over the world. We are very well aware that no one can resist our innocent look, which just shines with happiness, curiosity, and playfulness.

INTELLIGENCE: 🐾🐾🐾🐾🐾
OBEDIENCE: 🐾🐾🐾
ACTIVITY: Dancers
GUARDING: 🐾🐾🐾🐾
BARKING: We will alert you of every visitor, even one as small as a fly.
FAMILY TYPE: We are loyal to our families.
IDEAL HOME: We appreciate our own dog bed in the house or in the garden. We love digging!

LARGE AND MEDIUM TERRIERS

THE KERRY BLUE TERRIER ➡➡

Just look at my soft blue fur like no other dog has! I'm the epitome of elegance. And I'm even suitable for people with allergies. I just need a lot of exercise—swimming, hunting, tracking, or jumping. Let's go!

⬅ THE BEDLINGTON TERRIER

Don't let my soft, curly, sheep-like coat fool you! I'm more of a wolf in sheep's clothing, and I don't go far for a bite. Other dogs better keep out of my way. I don't mind other animals, as long as I grew up around them, or they don't try to run away from from me. That triggers my hunting instinct ... Don't forget to give me a haircut every three months.

AIREDALE TERRIER

IRISH TERRIER

AIREDALE AND ← IRISH TERRIERS

I'm the calmest of all terriers. I'm tough, brave, and very patient with children. I share these qualities with the Irish Terrier, even though he used to hunt tigers and lions! I'm not surprised that the Irish is called "the red devil" for being so brave and fearless. However, he is friendly and kind with his family and always keeps an eye on unwanted guests. When it comes to our training, be playful! We love to learn, but repeating the same command over and over? Running around sounds more fun.

SMOOTH FOX TERRIER AND WIRE FOX TERRIER →→

Don't be fooled by our innocent puppy-like expression. We have a mind of our own and can be pretty willful and stubborn. If we don't feel like sitting, we just won't and there is nothing you can do about it. But an experienced owner will know how to deal with us. If you are looking for a fast and energetic dog with a sense of humor, you came to the right place.

WIRE AND SMOOTH

← THE MANCHESTER TERRIER

Ok, I'm going to be honest: I like to bark. I bark when I'm happy, I bark when I'm sad, and I bark to alert you. There are many reasons to bark! But I'm sure you will forgive me: with my playful nature, one cannot stay mad at me for too long. I'm smart and energetic and I like to live in a pack. But what I really need is exercise and company. Don't leave me bored and alone ... You wouldn't do that to me, would you?

THE WELSH TERRIER ➛

I'll admit it even without a treat—I can act a little bossy around other dogs. I am, of course, considered the ancestor of all British terriers, and that should mean something. I bet you think, "Ha, this one is not going to be much fun!" On the contrary! Thanks to my lively and playful nature, you will change your mind quite quickly and even beg me to let you catch a breath, even when I'm old and gray!

SMALL TERRIERS

← JACK RUSSELL TERRIER

You want me to lie down on a couch? Yeah right, like that's going to happen! I'm energetic and hard-working and I was born to be an athlete and a hunter. If I can't burrow, I will at least dig you a nice hole in your garden that will make moles go green with envy. Let's go for a run or a bicycle ride or I'll entertain myself—furniture, get ready! I'm an expert on destruction and I will bark you a song! Woof!

WEST HIGHLAND WHITE TERRIER ➛

Cover your ears, I'm coming, woof! I'm full of energy, cheerful, friendly, and bold. I like to entertain people around me with my tricks, but I can also entertain myself with some toys. Although I was born to be a hunter, I can get used to city life. Get me involved in dog sports, and I'll show you what I can do! Just try it and throw me a ball or we can play tug-of-war. And if you let me run around and play with my family, I will be the happiest dog on earth!

DOGS' DAILY POST

298th YEAR — VOLUME 1 🐾 No. 3558 🐾 SATURDAY, JANUARY 1, 1910 🐾 35 DOG HAIRS

NiPPER, THE DOG FROM A PAINTING

Barking About Art

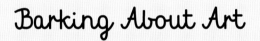

Nipper the dog sits by a big old gramophone with a shiny horn, with his snout pointing toward the mouth of that sonorous tube, listening carefully and patiently awaiting His Master's Voice. That's actually the name the English artist Francis Barraud gave to his painting of the doggy.

Probably a half-breed of a Jack Russell Terrier, the sad and forlorn little tramp, Nipper, was adopted by the painter's brother, Marc. Every evening, the grateful puppy and the content man would sit together and carefully listen to the music playing from one of the first gramophones ever. Unfortunately, after three years, Nipper became an orphan once again when Marc suddenly passed away.

For some time, he and the old gramophone stayed with Francis—it was right there where the artist noticed that whenever he turned on the gramophone, the dog would freeze, stop moving, and—almost as hypnotized—stare into the tube. It was if he was waiting for Mark to appear and for their lives to get back to normal.

Nipper wasn't just an ordinary dog, and Francis remembered him long after his dog pal set off for dog heaven. Or perhaps Nipper's ghost secretly visited him—how else would you explain that the painter decided to eternalize him in the painting His Master's Voice? The picture of Nipper intently listening to an old gramophone made it big printed on vinyl discs.

~ Atos and Brut ~

DOGS' DAILY POST

261st YEAR — VOLUME 11 🐾 No. 3124 🐾 SATURDAY, NOVEMBER 15, 1873 🐾 35 DOG HAIRS

GREYFRIARS BOBBY, THE NIGHT WATCHMAN

The stories of some dogs can be so moving that our two-legged friends can write about them in newspapers and magazines. One of such cases is the fate of a Skye Terrier named Bobby. Read an article about his life, recently published in the human magazine Me, Myself, and Dog.

This cute little Skye Terrier was brought into the family of John Gray, who had moved to Edinburgh in 1850 and started earning his daily bread as a city police night watchman. The master and his dog would walk together through murky alleys and keep a close eye on their safety. They didn't care whether winters were brisk or biting and didn't mind the summer heat or the fall rain because they were having a good time together and that was what mattered.

In February 1858, however, John Gray died of tuberculosis. He was buried in the Greyfriars cemetery and everyone was supposed to move on. But his loyal dog, Bobby, sat at his master's grave and waited. The grave-keeper's efforts to chase him away were fruitless; Bobby would always come back, whether the sun was glaring down or it was raining cats and dogs or whether it was freezing or snowing. Bobby wouldn't leave his spot for an incredible 14 years.

Good people would bring him food and take care of him. After he passed away, they made him a statue so Bobby and his unconditional dog love and loyalty would never be forgotten.

Stories of genuine friendship

CAIRN TERRIER ➡

I have the soul of a hunter. Even if I'm perfectly trained and walk next to you like a good boy, the second I see a squirrel I'm gone. It's safer to walk me on a lead, especially in the city. I need exercise, as all terriers do. And if you exercise with me, I will love you to the moon and back. The bigger the family, the better! I will always be by your side!

SCOTTISH TERRIER ⬅

Grr, I may be little, but I'm good at guarding. My motto is: you cannot be careful enough. I'm cautious around strangers—it takes me some time to trust someone. I'm stubborn and have a mind of my own, so please have patience with me. Even one of the previous presidents of the United States of America, Franklin D. Roosevelt, fell in love with one of my ancestors, and now they rest together.

BORDER TERRIER ➡

You wanna go for a run? I'm coming with you. You want to just lie down on a couch? I'm in! Are you planning a weekend trip to the mountains? Well then don't forget to pack my dog food. I will do anything your heart desires; I'm not stubborn at all. That means I'm a good choice even for beginners. I know what you're thinking: you just found the dog of your dreams!

OTHER SMALL TERRIERS

1. SKYE TERRIER: I come from Scotland and I was the favorite of the Queen of England Victoria herself! There are not many of us left, so take good care of us and protect us at all costs.

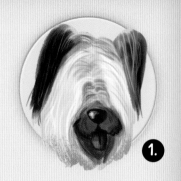

2. AUSTRALIAN TERRIER: Grr, I'm not afraid of anything or anyone! I'm not afraid of rodents, venomous snakes, or even ... cats!

3. GERMAN HUNTING TERRIER (JAGDTERRIER): I excel at burrow hunting competitions. Foxes, get ready!

4. DANDIE DINMONT TERRIER: Even with my shaggy hairstyle, I'm presentable in every situation. And I was named by the great writer Walter Scott himself!

5. NORFOLK TERRIER: In the good old days, I used to chase rats around that renowned English university in Cambridge. Yes, I'm such a brave, good boy.

BULL-TYPE TERRIERS

BULL TERRIER ➡

Grr, I used to be the gladiator of the dog world ... I have a big and muscular body and my ancestors used to fight in dog fighting pits to the death. But over time, I became a peaceful, patient, and gentle dog, and even children are my friends! I will tolerate it even if they sometimes affectionately pull my ears.

STAFFORDSHiRE BULL TERRiER ➡

I'm somewhat of a bodybuilder: big, muscular, and renowned for my bravery and willfulness. I can hold prey larger than myself with my teeth. I used to excel in bull fights, so people are often surprised by how gentle, loving, and playful I am. I have unconditional love for my family, especially the kids. I will gladly share my bed with you—I really don't like being alone.

← AMERiCAN PiT BULL TERRiER

I used to be the best in the dog fighting pits, but luckily, those are finally forbidden. I mean, who would want to fight their friends all the time? But some of those instincts are still in my blood or, well, in my genes. When we are on a walk and meet other dogs, I might want to prove I'm bigger, stronger, louder, and dominant, grr! You need to start introducing me to other dogs, people, and different situations since puppyhood so I can get used to them. With the right upbringing, I will love you more than any squeaky ball and I will do everything for you.

AMERiCAN STAFFORDSHiRE TERRiER ➡

Some dogs may not be very eager to work, but that's not me. I love retrieving, tracking, and protection training. I'm born to be the guardian of my family. Thieves are intimidated by my looks alone because I'm full of muscles. I can be a little restless because of my curiosity.

TOY TERRIERS

YORKSHIRE TERRIER ➡

A bow on one's head, a velvet pillow, a cozy apartment, and a loving owner—what more can one wish for? Comfort and luxury look good on us! We used to live, however, with the English poor in the eleventh century because only the rich could afford big hunting dogs. We would not be able to chase the deer with those little feet of ours! But rats, they tremble with fear to this day, bow-wow! We are excellent at catching rats! Although it is not all that obvious, we do need a firm hand that can handle our legendary stubbornness. Oh, and if we scrounge for something, don't give in to our sad eyes—we tend to gain weight. Woof-woof!

⬅ AUSTRALIAN SILKY TERRIER

We'll be waiting for you all day long in your warm house—the couch is great to lie on! But when you get back from work or school, we're ready for action. Doing sports, fooling around, chasing, walking, running ... it's up to you and your interests. We can adapt perfectly to the young and old. We look like cuddly toys, but are also full of life and boldness! If somebody does you wrong, they should watch out! We will intervene immediately. Vrrr!

ENGLISH TOY TERRIER ➡

Woof-woof! Some of us may bark a little more than you might like, but don't blame us. We will protect you and your property as if our life depended on it. Not only are we great guards, but also joyful friends for life. However, if you want to have mice, hamsters, or rats at home along with us, we have to warn you in advance. Keep them away from us as we are naturally inclined to fight with these animals without hesitation. I mean, we were originally rodent hunters, so we simply cannot escape it.

DOGS' POST

DAILY

388th YEAR — VOLUME 3 ❖ No. 4640 ❖ THURSDAY, MARCH 2, 2000 ❖ 35 DOG HAIRS

CRISSCROSSING AFRICA WITH BULL TERRIER JOCK

JOCK OF THE BUSHVELD, THE BOOK ABOUT THE WELL-TRAVELED BULL TERRIER JOCK, HAS BEEN THE TOP PUPPY BESTSELLER FOR YEARS. AND SINCE WE ARE LITERALLY BOMBARDED WITH YOUR REQUESTS TO PUBLISH AN INTERVIEW WITH THE AUTHOR—JAMES PERCY FITZPATRICK, WHO BECAME FAMOUS THANKS TO JOCK—HERE IT IS!!

Mr. FitzPatrick, how did you meet Jock?
When the gold rush broke out in the nineteenth century in South Africa, I thought it was worth checking it out. Soon after my arrival, a dog in our camp gave birth to six puppies. Five of them were big and strong, but the sixth was weak and didn't stand a chance of surviving without help. What could one do? I took care of the puppy, and that's how I met Jock. Although I didn't find any gold, I found a buddy for life.

What can you say about Jock?
Jock was an absolutely wonderful dog. He was nice, friendly, loving, brave, intelligent, and well-behaved. He traveled the length and breadth of South Africa with me. Yes, we went through a lot together. He taught me how to live in harmony with nature, which has become so close to my heart. He kept me company on cold nights, accompanied me on every adventure, and helped me guard the little I carried with me.

Did you know back then that you would write a children's book about your stories?
Not yet. My four children talked me into it. Every time they went to bed, they wanted me to tell a bedtime story about Jock. They enjoyed the stories so much that I created a whole book for them in 1907. And Jock, the brave, incredibly kind, and loyal dog, now lives in these stories forever.

MY DOG SKIP AND ME!

BARK FOR A FAMILY TICKET IN ADVANCE!

Will is a shy and timid little boy, who has no siblings or friends to play with. Fortunately, he has a bold Wire Fox Terrier Skip and together, they can stay brave enough to spend the night in a haunted cemetery!

TOTO OF OZ

Heroes of World-Famous Stories

Which of our puppies would not know the story of Dorothy of Oz and does not have a poster of their fairy-tale idol, Dorothy's dog Toto, the small Cairn terrier, on the wall? Let's have a look at a primary school class in which students are rehearsing a play about Toto and his friend.

Fido: I am dachshund Fido and I play the role of Toto. Together with the teacher, we've made Toto's furry coat. I like it the most when Dorothy and I are picked up by the tornado and fly to the East.

Marley: I am Maltese Marley and play the role of Dorothy. I'd rather try the role of Toto, even though I'm a girl. As a dog, I'd understand him better, that's for sure.

Teacher and director in one: Our school focused on the story of Dorothy of Oz because it is extremely popular among puppy generations. However, we emphasized Toto's character—in our version, he is the one who leads Dorothy to the Wizard.

Fido: I want to be like Toto one day, so brave ... And I'd also like to have a master like Dorothy. She must be fun!

YORKSHIRE TERRIER SMOKY

The "Dog Heroines" SERIES

You don't need to be really big or strong as a Great Dane to be able to save the world or your master. The small Yorkshire Terrier Smokey, who was only 18 cm tall and weighed less than 2 kilograms, is proof of that!

This cute foundling actually became a war heroine during World War II. Aboard a military aircraft alongside her soldier master William A. Wynne, she took part in 12 air and sea rescue missions and was awarded 8 battle stars for them. This tiny lady managed to survive with ease and no injuries 150 terrifying air stri-kes targeted at New Guinea and lift the mood of the miserable soldiers at the same time.

Ta-ta-ta-dah! Let the triumphant fanfares be heard! In fact, it was Smokey who helped connect the telegraph wires used by airmen to communicate with their military headquarters. It wasn't an easy task at all: she had to run through an 8-in wide and 68-ft long underground tunnel with a cable attached to her collar. Some parts of the tunnel were even blocked by soil. It was clear that no soldier could accomplish this mission. Only Smokey could stretch the cable with ease and save her entire unit. "She taught me just as much as I taught her," Wynne used to say with a smile. Smokey simply proves that even small female dogs can achieve great things!

SHEEPDOGS AND CATTLE DOGS

We've always helped people manage their flocks of sheep. We herded the large flocks to prevent sheep from running away, and when there was a sheep on the run, we chased after it and made it rejoin the flock. We, sheepdogs and cattle dogs breeds, are very bright and we like working— it brings us joy. We are persistent, fast, and tough, and when you train us, we listen to your commands. In order for the sheep to respect us, we must also be stern and strict. We don't mind the whims of the weather. We love people, and our loyalty will continue beyond the grave.

SHEEPDOGS

CZECHOSLOVAKIAN WOLFDOG ➤

I'll be honest; it's not easy with me. I am quick to learn, lively, loyal, persistent, fearless ... Only a strong master can tame me, a strong pack leader. I am half wolf, wild, and independent. I rarely bark, but I can howl loudly when I do not like something or if I miss my owner.

← KOMONDOR (HUNGARIAN SHEEPDOG)

I look like I'm sleeping and lazing about, but that's a mistake! Don't underestimate me! I am secretly on guard watching everything, so all trespassers better watch their step! But I'm more of a peaceful dog than a wild one, which has to constantly run everywhere and jump. My coat looks like twine and protects me perfectly, whether it's pouring, freezing, or the wind is blowing outside. So I am an all-weather dog.

Woof, grrr, woof, I'm a shepherd who knows its worth. When I have a good teacher, I learn everything he wants from me and learn it very quickly. I'm a tough cookie. I'm not afraid of anyone or anything. If you want me to live with you, we have to go outside for a jog and jump around all the time. I'm very hardworking. If nothing happens for a long time and I have nothing to do, grrr, I can even be a bad dog.

GERMAN SHEPHERD

INTELLIGENCE: 🐾🐾🐾🐾🐾

OBEDIENCE: 🐾🐾🐾

ACTIVITY: Hard workers

GUARDING: 🐾🐾🐾🐾🐾

BARKING: By barking, we immediately tell you how we feel.

FAMILY TYPE: Protecting our owner is our duty!

IDEAL HOME: The more space, the better!

BELGIAN SHEPHERD →

Grrrrr ... Watch out if you're a stranger! I'm a defender: I put my heart and soul into everything, so for me, everybody is a suspect in advance. I'm not a villain—it's just in my blood. I am very sensitive and attentive to my family members. But you have to have a way with me. It's impossible to handle me without proper training!

← BEAUCERON

I want everyone to be straight with me and treat me equally! You are not superior, and I am not inferior! And when you get me, don't give me to anyone else; separation or a complete change of owner can break my heart, no matter how tough I might look!

WELSH CORGI

INTELLIGENCE: 🐾🐾🐾🐾🐾

OBEDIENCE: 🐾🐾🐾🐾🐾
(We are quick learners!)

ACTIVITY: Recreational athletes
(We love to chase a ball!)

GUARDING: 🐾🐾🐾

BARKING: We are no yappers but bark when excited!

FAMILY TYPE: We can get used to other pets but not to unfamiliar dogs or cats.

IDEAL HOME: We don't mind a flat but need an active owner!

WELSH CORGI

We are small, but we are not afraid of anything. The person who gets us will have a faithful and patient friend in us and absolutely reliable guards. Although we like all people, not every dog is nice to us and sometimes, we just don't understand them. We love taking walks and getting some fresh air, but long mountain hikes are not for us—after all, we have quite short legs! Oh, and one more thing: aggression is not in our nature.

COLLIE

Although we are considered the best herding dog breed in the world, we look more like aristocrats than diligent servants. We have an extraordinary sense of humor. If there is fun, we'll be there too. We love play. Woof! If you want to have us at home, prepare yourself for regular grooming. We like to run and walk, but if our owner is not an active person, we can easily adapt to his idle style.

BEARDED COLLIE

BORDER COLLIE

ROUGH COLLIE

COLLIE

INTELLIGENCE: 🐾🐾🐾🐾🐾

OBEDIENCE: 🐾🐾🐾 (We are enthusiastic learners!)

ACTIVITY: Tireless (Are you up for a game? Please, please, please!)

GUARDING: 🐾🐾🐾🐾🐾

BARKING: We just have a lot to say!

FAMILY TYPE: Everyone who throws the ball, we are loyal to you!

IDEAL HOME: Plains and meadows for a good run, that's what we like.

DOGS' POST

DAILY

397th YEAR — VOLUME 7 ❧ No. 4752 ❧ WEDNESDAY, JULY 22, 2009 ❧ 35 DOG HAIRS

RIN TIN TIN

In 1922, we signed a contract with one of the major film studios and I began to play the leading roles. And I was great. Over time, I became a real star. I had a personal chef who prepared me delicacies, my wage was $ 6,000 a week, and I received honorary keys to the city of New York. My life, which began so darkly in the muddy ruins of war in France, turned into a fairy-tale.

And if I hadn't been a dog, I would have won an Oscar. But you know people—rather than rewarding animals, they quickly changed the rules and the Academy Award for Best Actor was stolen from me by a biped named Emil Jannings.

FOR ALL THE LOVERS OF STARS OF THE SILVER SCREEN, GOLDIE PAW, THE ART EDITOR AT THE DOGS' POST DAILY, PREPARED A SHORT RECOLLECTION OF RIN TIN TIN, THE FAMOUS ACTOR OF THE GERMAN SHEPHERD FAMILY.

If it wasn't for the soldier Lee Duncan, I would have never gotten the chance to be an actor. Lee Duncan helped me big time. As a little naive puppy, he rescued me in France from the ruins of a bombed village, then drove me to America and began training me for the film industry. We got the ball rolling.

BOB THE RAILWAY DOG

life as good as a travel

It's summer and summer means travel—by car, bus, plane, or train. Today, in our issue, we will focus on trains and their loyal fan, Bob The Railway Collie, a dog who spent all his earthly life on the rails. More precisely, on the coal storage car of a steam locomotive, which was his favorite place. Let us take you on a ride, but make sure you don't take his seat!

Believe it or not, our Bob didn't get to board every passenger car. Such suburban trains did not suit him: they were too confined for his liking. He did not turn up his snout, however, at third class. He loved it when the train was puffing and chugging and the train driver cheerfully sang. After all, these guys were his dear friends and on top of that, they were giving him a ride for free ...

To those doggies that love to bark, growl, and snarl, take an example from your ancestor, old Bob Railway (1882 – 1895), and run to all the stations of the world, jump into high-speed, inter-city, and super express trains or even the Orient Express and show people how dogs can travel!

~ Frank S. Team ~

I'm sure you're thinking that this lucky Bob must have had a pretty adventurous owner. But you're wrong. Bob was traveling alone. He simply left his owner one day and followed his curious snout, which led him to the station. There, he bursted with love for trains. Although some good souls brought him home three times, since the age of nine months, our dog adventurer happily traveled around South Australia.

OTHER SHEEPDOGS AND CATTLE DOGS

1. AUSTRALIAN SHEPHERD: If anyone is looking for a really devoted dog, bingo! Here I am. But my owner better not be a layabout! I have a lot of energy that needs to get out, otherwise I will get bored. Then, I might destroy things around me and bark unreasonably all day long. You know, idle hands are the devil's playground.

2. WHITE SWISS SHEPHERD: What other dogs don't even feel hurts me, so you have to be very careful with me. On the other hand, the cold and bad weather don't bother me at all.

3. BERGAMASCO SHEPHERD: I have wild Italian blood flowing in my veins. I live simply and love having company. I can do any work perfectly, but as soon as it's the end of my shift, I have to rest properly. You know, siesta!

4. BRIARD (FRENCH SHEPHERD): As a good Frenchman, I like fashion fads, so don't wonder at my long bangs that cover both of my eyes. I love getting up to mischief and having fun, and I don't care if I'm a puppy or an adult.

5. PICARDY SHEPHERD: I look like an uncombed cute little dog, but at the core, I'm a real rascal. I can be really hard-headed, and I'm definitely the most stubborn of all the dog breeds.

6. SCHIPPERKE: Is there another more curious breed than us, schipperkes? No way, perhaps only just as curious as us! We also love to beg for something on your table until we get it. Yum.

7. PUMI: I need freedom and room for running and carefree barking. I like to bark, and I like to do it often, so be prepared. I am also said to be intelligent.

BOBTAIL (OLD ENGLISH SHEEPDOG) ➡➡

We look like big cute stuffed animals ... We don't like violence, we are kind, playful, devoted, and social, and and never say no to fun. Because of this kind nature, even a beginner dog owner can have us. We listen to your commands even without hard training; we are simply happy when our owner is happy. We need to lead an active life, however, with an active lifestyle and a loving approach.

⬅ AUSTRALIAN KELPIE

Work and work again, I can't help it ... Grrr, but I have to have something to do all the time: running around, jumping ... Boredom makes me nervous, yuck! Living in the country with an active owner at my side is my fulfilled Kelpian dream. Woof!

CATTLE DOGS

AUSTRALIAN CATTLE DOG ➡➡

You know, we're kind of detached from people we don't know. We believe in the saying "trust, but verify." But we are loyal to our owner and want to be wherever they are. We have a sixth sense, which tells us all their feelings, displeasure or joy, sympathy or antipathy. And being the hard workers we are, if we were human, we would be called workaholics.

AUSTRALIAN CATTLE DOG

INTELLIGENCE: 🐾🐾🐾🐾🐾

OBEDIENCE: 🐾🐾 (It's not easy to train us.)

ACTIVITY: Chasers (Our schedule: 2 hours a day outside!)

GUARDING: 🐾🐾🐾🐾

BARKING: Prepare for our frequent and intense, high-pitched barks!

FAMILY TYPE: We need to get used to children from our early age.

IDEAL HOME: Farm

MARTHA MY DEAR

PAUL McCARTNEY

Only a few dogs can boast of becoming the protagonist of a successful song!

Old English Sheepdog Martha, a four-legged beauty, charmed Paul McCartney himself—the bassist of the legendary English band The Beatles—at first sight. This happened in 1966, the year of her birth. Paul bought the cute puppy, a fluffy ball, and took it with his partner to their London flat.

The moments when the famous musician would play with him and pet him were some of the most important and essential memories of his life. You know, even people can sometimes love as unconditionally as we, dogs, do.

Well, even every little puppy that still has milk on its whiskers knows that love, the greatest emotion, is also the source of the greatest inspiration in artists. That's why Paul McCartney composed the song Martha My Dear. And a few years later, a photo of one of Martha's puppies adorned the cover of the entire song album!

DOGS' POST

Daily

407th YEAR — VOLUME 8 ❖ No. 4871 ❖ SUNDAY, AUGUST 18, 2019 ❖ 35 DOG HAIRS

THE ROYAL CORGIS

Some dogs are great drovers, others are perfect hunters, and then there are those that rank among the best guard dogs in the world. But only some dog breeds can be described as truly "royal." Let's have a look at corgis, little dogs, which won the heart of Queen Elizabeth II herself.

The royal family fell in love with the aristocratic corgis back in the 1930s. It is therefore not surprising that for her 18th birthday, Elizabeth II received a dog of this breed. She started calling her Susan.

The young Queen immediately grew fond of this little furry dog with short legs and mischievous ideas. Susan even came along on her honeymoon in 1947. Secretly, of course, so that no one knew.

Since then, Queen Elizabeth has been constantly surrounded by playful corgis. Some of them were even Susan's offsprings. Can you believe that the Queen of England bred thirty corgis over this long period?

And why not! Corgis, which have literally become symbols of the British Kingdom, are not an ordinary breed.

They come from around the twelfth century AD and have been excellent trackers, herders, hunters, and guards from the dawn of their history. These days, as enthusiastic athletes always glowing and in a cheerful mood, they are great companions, appreciated even by the Queen.

🐾 THE TALE OF SWANSEA JACK 🐾

The "Dog Heroes" SERIES

DEAR PUPPIES, IT SOMETIMES HAPPENS THAT YOUR DOG CAREER DOESN'T TAKE OFF EXACTLY HOW YOU OR YOUR HUMAN MASTERS IMAGINED . . . YOU MIGHT, FOR EXAMPLE, LOSE YOUR COOL AND JUMP RIGHT IN A LAKE FULL OF DUCKS. BUT DON'T WORRY ABOUT IT, BECAUSE NOT EVEN THIS HAS TO STOP YOU FROM BECOMING A RISING STAR AND ACHIEVING GREAT SUCCESS. JUST HOW IT DIDN'T STOP THE LEGENDARY SWANSEA JACK.

Once upon a time, in the seaport city of Swansea in Wales, lived one Labrador Retriever, whose name was Swansea Jack. His first master gave up on him when Jack attacked some ducks that were splashing around on the lake. "I don't want a troublemaker like that!" he said to himself and sent Jack away.

Luckily, Jack found a new master, William Thomas, who started teaching him how to save drowning people and drag them out of the water. Jack would simply swim up to the poor person, grab their swimming suit or shirt, and then pull them to the shore.

From 1931, when he became a "professional lifeguard," up until the end of his life, Jack dragged 27 drowning Welsh out of the water! (You know, back then people couldn't really swim . . .) For his great service, he was awarded a silver collar, a silver cup, and even two bronze medals.

Jack's first owner, Mr. Taulford Davies, surely never forgave himself for judging Jack so quickly. Such a great dog with lots of courage and an even bigger heart!

RETRiEVERS, FLUSHiNG, AND WATER DOGS

Splish splash! Are you trying to get us out of the water? Splash! There's no use in trying—we, water dogs, are almost like fish; water is our element! Don't worry, on land, we'll listen to your every word. I'll shake my paw on it! We are friendly, kind, and smart by nature—you won't find fighters among us. Flushing dogs will appreciate, however, some hunting training, in which they can apply their tracking skills.

INTELLIGENCE: 🐾🐾🐾🐾🐾

OBEDIENCE: 🐾🐾🐾🐾🐾

ACTIVITY: Playful pet (We need to jump, swim, run, shake, and cuddle all our energy away!)

GUARDING: 🐾🐾🐾

BARKING: We alert you when we see prey or visitors.

FAMILY TYPE: We are loyal and faithful to our family.

IDEAL HOME: House by the lake

RETRiEVERS

CURLY-COATED RETRiEVER AND FLAT-COATED RETRiEVER ➡

We love when the wind raises our ears as we run and when our fur is wet through and through after frolicking in the water! Even at the age of three, we still act like big puppies. And even in old age, we won't turn into grumpy old sourpusses. My curly friend has a bit more of a tumultuous natur and needs stronger leadership. With training, he can also become a great companion to an active family.

CURLY-COATED RETRIEVER

FLAT-COATED RETRIEVER

⬅ LABRADOR

Do you know what assistance dog training looks like? I learn how to bring all kinds of things right to my master's hands as early as puppyhood. I, myself, bring them the lead; I press the button at the crosswalk, take out the laundry from the washing machine, or bring them their cell phone. Helping people is my mission! I'll gladly help you too, even if you don't have any special needs. We'll make a great team. Just be careful not to spoil me too much with dog treats—I tend to get overweight.

GOLDEN RETRiEVER

My kind expression tells you a lot about my nature. I am good to the core and can easily empathize with people and understand them. Just like Labradors, you can see me alongside blind people as a reliable assistance dog. In my free time, I like to play with kids. I need plenty of movement in my life. So put on your sneakers, we're going out!

FLUSHiNG DOGS

CLUMBER SPANiEL ➡

Compared to other Spaniels, I don't have high demands for movement. But don't you dare say that it shows on my figure! Yes, I'm a bit cumbersome, I have a tendency to get fat, and I'm not among the fastest dogs, but my perseverance is comparable to that of any marathon runner!

ENGLiSH SPRiNGER SPANiEL AND WELSH SPRiNGER SPANiEL

Yay, look, water! Plop, and we're in it up to our ears. We're pros at finding water! We love to race with fish to see who can swim longer. You can call on us all you want, but as soon as we see water, catch a trail, or see a bird, our hunting instincts kick in. You'll have to be patient with us, but in return, we'll reward you for it with unconditional love and affection.

WELSH SPRINGER SPANIEL

ENGLISH SPRINGER SPANIEL

DOGS' POST

DAILY

394th YEAR — VOLUME 11 ❖ No. 4720 ❖ SUNDAY, NOVEMBER 5, 2006 ❖ 35 DOG HAIRS

FROM THE DIARY OF MERLIN THE SPRINGER SPANIEL

Tales from history that actually happened

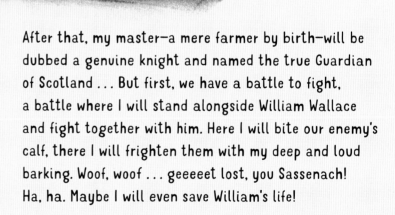

11 September 1297

The sun is slowly rising in the sky, but I can feel in my canine bones the fall coming. My master William Wallace, Scottish with all his heart and soul, is a little bit uneasy and he has good reason for being so! In the series of struggles for Scottish independence, an extremely important battle—the Battle of Stirling Bridge—lies ahead of him.

He paces around the military camp and strokes me on the head from time to time. Perhaps I should be a little nervous too, but I'm not. As a proper Springer Spaniel, I can foresee the future. I know this battle will be victorious for my master and that the English will get their lumps.

After that, my master—a mere farmer by birth—will be dubbed a genuine knight and named the true Guardian of Scotland ... But first, we have a battle to fight, a battle where I will stand alongside William Wallace and fight together with him. Here I will bite our enemy's calf, there I will frighten them with my deep and loud barking. Woof, woof ... geeeeet lost, you Sassenach! Ha, ha. Maybe I will even save William's life!

But let's leave that for now: the sun is still rising. I'll fix myself some raw meat for breakfast, run around the camp, stretch my muscles, and then we'll go—me, Merlin the Springer Spaniel, and my master William Wallace.

RUN, HONEY, RUN!

IF YOU THINK THAT YOU HAVE TO REACH A CERTAIN AGE TO SAVE A HUMAN IN DANGER, YOU CAN'T BE MORE WRONG. SOMETIMES, EVEN A RATHER YOUNG PUPPY CAN HAVE SOME COURAGE AND ITS HEART IN THE RIGHT PLACE. ALL YOU HAVE TO DO IS MENTION THE NAME HONEY, AND THE DOG PUBLIC WILL KNOW.

See for yourself in a survey we took on the streets of both bigger and smaller cities.

Does the name "Honey" ring a bell?
Andy (8 years): Honey? Ummmmwrr ... Do you mean that little five-month-old Cocker Spaniel puppy who saved her master after they'd been in a car accident?

Yes, that's exactly what we mean.
Andy (8 years): I admit, she was and still is a brave lady! I can't imagine the shock, lying in an upside-down car in an 80-feet deep ravine, not knowing what's going on ... Sorry, I have go now, my master is calling for me!

Patty (2 years): Oh, Honey? I have nothing but admiration for her! She got stuck with her master in a rolled-over car. Her master got her out through a small gap and Honey ran for help. Incredibly powerful story!

Black (1 year): It's said that a five-month-old puppy ran a good half a mile to get help. Half a mile in a completely strange area! You see what I mean? I am half a year older, but I couldn't imagine doing that.

Sparky (3.5 years): Honey is my little hero. Only thanks to her courage and keeping a cool head her master survived. She ran to some people and barked so desperately that they realized something wasn't right. If it wasn't it for her, her master would be long gone. In my opinion, Honey deserves a proper reward, like a statue or a chain of sausages!

ENGLISH COCKER SPANIEL AND AMERICAN COCKER SPANIEL ➤➤

If you like to sit on a couch, we'll adapt to you, but then don't be surprised when we get fat! You know, dogs mirror the owners' personalities. You will find great friends in us Cockers. We're friendly, good-tempered, curious, and full of energy. We were originally hunters, and even nowadays, we need a lot of movement—especially English Cocker Spaniels, who have maintained their passion for hunting and who feel at home in the woods. I, the American Cocker Spaniel, love to gain points at dog shows and dog sports. Don't forget to comb our fur and clean our ears.

AMERICAN COCKER SPANIEL

ENGLISH COCKER SPANIEL

← FIELD SPANIEL

Woof, let's play! I'm a gentle and intelligent dog, who is able to get along with everybody. When I fall in love with you, I'll stay by your side till death do us part and lick your nose up to your eyebrows. My back and shoulders are all muscle. That's why I'm a good flushing dog, and I will bring any prey right under your nose. Especially hunters will appreciate that. Otherwise, I am a simple dog who enjoys life in the country. I don't really fit into cities.

GERMAN SPANIEL ➤➤

My motto is: always be ready! I will track down every quail hidden in the grass, every hare disguised as a clump of dirt, and even treats hidden in your pockets. There are so many delicious smells in the world! No wonder I'm always in a good mood and full of energy. Hunters love me.

WATER DOGS

WETTERHOUN →

I have tracked down many rabbits, otters, and other small animals during my life. I'm a calm, intelligent, and a brave gun dog and a good swimmer. Raising me is difficult. I have my own head, and I can get pretty stubborn. Be careful not to become my pet, he he! As my owners, you will need a lot of patience and will-power, but you'll get a reward for it: me!

BARBET

SPANISH WATER DOG

PORTUGUESE WATER DOG

↑ PORTUGUESE, BARBET, AND SPANISH WATER DOGS

Look, a fish! Splash, and it's ours. In the past, we were invaluable helpers to fishermen. As great swimmers and divers, we helped them haul the fishing nets, delivered messages from ships to land, saved people who were drowning, and defended them and their families from all the dangers they faced at sea at the time

(including pirates). Oof, that was a lot of work! We are intelligent, bright, and also obedient. We love children, and Spaniels in particular need to be constantly in contact with their family. The Barbet will amaze you with its webbed feet, while the Portuguese Water Dog is suitable for people with allergies. We all do well in the country.

OTHER RETRIEVERS

1. NOVA SCOTIA DUCK TOLLING RETRIEVER: I am a great hunter, companion, and an assistance dog. I am also very handsome.

2. CHESAPEAKE BAY RETRIEVER: My youth tends to be wild. But when you provide me with hunting training or other activities, I calm down.

3. KOOIKERHONDJE: I am friendly, even though ducks would disagree . . .

4. SUSSEX SPANIEL: I am not especially fast but, thanks to my endurance, can be a great companion even on mountain hikes.

5. LAGOTTO ROMAGNOLO: I dig better than moles! I have a very sensitive nose—I can also be used as a truffle hunter.

AMERICAN AND IRISH WATER SPANIEL ➜

Our thick and curly coat protects us from cold water, thorns, and thistles. We are hunting dogs and will jump in the water for many caught ducks or even just for a stick—just for fun! We're happiest alongside brave watermen, but if you suggest another dog sport, we will gladly follow you. We are kind and affectionate toward our loved ones but wary of strangers. Growl.

IRISH WATER SPANIEL

AMERICAN WATER SPANIEL

MiSSY KELSEY, THE GOLDEN RETRiEVER

The "Dog Heroines" SERIES

The end of the year is a time of miracles, as the human Bob can tell you. He almost died on New Year's Eve in the far, far away town of Petoskey, Michigan only to quickly "come back to life." And who does he have to thank for his life? His beloved dog, the Golden Retriever girl with a beautiful name—Kelsey.

"My master was cold that afternoon . . . So he decided to get a couple of logs to light up the fire in the fireplace. He ran out wearing just sweatpants, a T-shirt, and slippers, even though it was freezing! What a bad idea, let me tell you . . . As any sensible dog, I tried to talk him out of it—I was whining—but he just wouldn't listen to me! Can you believe that? 'I'll be right back,' he said.

Along the way, however, he slipped and injured his spine. He called for help until it grew dark, but in the midst of the celebrations and the noise from all those bright fireworks (which we, dogs, don't like all that much), nobody could hear him. Fortunately, I did hear him and ran to him in an instant. I lied on top of him to keep him from freezing to death, every now and then licked his face, and most importantly, I barked for dear life so that someone would hear us and come save my master.

Only in the morning, after an endless nineteen hours, did the neighbor finally hear my barking and howling and came out to see what was happening. In the meantime, Bob lost consciousness and I was worried about him. He had to live; he couldn't die! I was crying inside. But Bob didn't let me down. At the hospital, he recovered incredibly quickly. I guess he wanted to return all my care and love. Woof!"

SPITZ
AND PRIMITIVE DOGS

Some of us are the kings of the north: bundled in thick warm fur, with pointed ears and a sharp muzzle peeking out. We are happy to run around in the forest and in a snow blizzard. If Santa's sleigh wasn't pulled by reindeer, he would have certainly chosen us. As a dog team, we are able to run many kilometres. The smaller of us could be a bit stubborn. After all, their ancestors were wolves too!

NORDIC SLED DOGS

INTELLIGENCE: 🐾🐾🐾🐾🐾

OBEDIENCE: 🐾🐾🐾🐾

ACTIVITY: Snow travelers

GUARDING: 🐾

BARKING: We rarely bark.

FAMILY TYPE: We will gladly warm you up in winter.

IDEAL HOME: We need a lot of space: a doghouse is not enough for us.

NORDIC SLED DOGS

SIBERIAN HUSKY

I don't get tired easily! I'm a dog sled champion. I'm fast, persistent, and open-minded. I'm a wanderer, but I still love company. I need to live in a pack with people or other dogs. I get along great with them and their pups. In the past, I used to warm the feet of the indigenous people in Siberia called the Chukchi—the good old days!

SIBERIAN HUSKY

ALASKAN MALAMUTE

SAMOYED

SAMOYED

Snow, snow, and snow everywhere . . . but is it? Can't you see the black ball? That's my nose. I got you! I know hundreds of games we can play in the snow. We'll pull together as a team: I have loads of experience with that. Since ancient times, I have helped tribes far north as a draft and hunting dog. I will gladly pull you on a sled! Hold tight to something: here we go!

ALASKAN MALAMUTE

You and me, we create a pack. If you want to be in charge, you can't be afraid and you have to be able to show us who is the boss. Kindly but vigorously and whining! We can ride bikes together, swim, or run long-distance races. If I don't do anything for a while, I'll get bored quickly and then you won't want to see what I can do with your sneakers . . . There's a possibility they will end up destroyed.

NORDIC HUNTING DOGS

From time to time, you people have taken us for overgrown furry pets. But you should know that we are hunters to the core. Show us who's the boss but respect us. Then you'll have a friend in us.

↑

WEST SIBERIAN LAIKA

My life is full of work and adventure. You can find me in the Ural region or Siberia, where I track and hunt bears, elk, and other large and small game. I can be used as a sled or guarding dog. Although I am fond of the whole family, I will only obey one master.

BLACK AND GRAY NORWEGIAN ELKHOUND

I have the wild blood of my fearless hunting ancestors flowing in my veins. They have been working on their unique hunting strategy for over 5,000 years! They chased elk, lynx, wolves, and even bears into advantageous locations and then called out for their masters with a loud bark. We are committed to man to this day. We love our family and we can protect it from the impact of snowflakes!

↓

NORDIC HUNTING DOGS

INTELLIGENCE: 🐾🐾🐾🐾🐾

OBEDIENCE: 🐾🐾🐾🐾🐾

ACTIVITY: Windcatchers (We need to feel the wind in our hair.)

GUARDING: 🐾🐾🐾🐾🐾

BARKING: There must be a good reason for us to bark: prey or a thief.

FAMILY TYPE: We will protect our family with our own life.

IDEAL HOME: A country house with everything that goes with it.

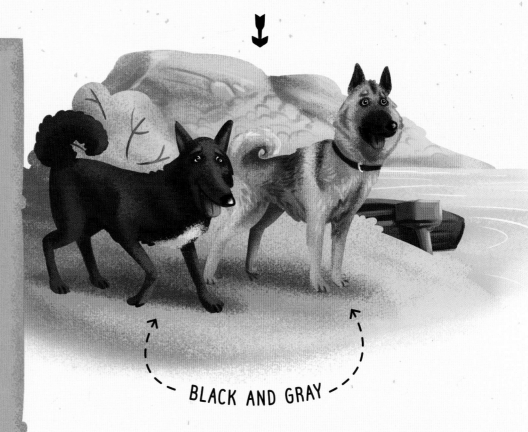

BLACK AND GRAY

HUSKY BALTO AND HIS TEAM SAVE AN ALASKAN TOWN

A unique memory of musher Gunnar Kaasen

We are in Alaska, where the regular great sled dog race in honor of the celebrated Husky Balto is about to begin. The mushers encourage their packs. Today's goal is to win a cup full of hot tea and a ring of sausages. Back in 1925, however, the aim was just to survive. You will learn more from the story of Gunnar Kaasen.

"The year 1925 was crazy here in Alaska. An epidemic of diphtheria spread in the town of Nome, and large numbers of people were dying. I lived thousands of miles away from the place, but together with other mushers, we decided to save Nome. We were determined to bring the life-saving vaccine to local people on the sled and fight all the vagaries of weather with our dogs.

The pack was led by Husky Balto. You know, I liked him, but he was ... Well, a dodo—slow and clumsy. No musher wanted him. But I believed in him. On the way there, we were caught in a snowstorm. I couldn't see my own glove, so I had no choice but to rely on Balto. The dog led us directly to our destination and even managed to avoid a dangerous unfrozen section of the Topkok River! That's how great he was!

We brought the vaccine in time and saved the people of Nome. And you surely know who helped us achieve that: Balto, of course, the outsider dog, who was mistrusted and laughed at by others, except for me. Bottom line, Balto was the best dog I've ever had!"

ZANDER AND HIS EXCELLENT NOSE

ZANDER IS A BEAUTIFUL SAMOYED-HUSKY MIX WITH FLUFFY WHITE HAIR. HIS MASTERS GOT HIM FROM A SHELTER WHEN HE WAS SEVEN YEARS OLD AND, SINCE THEN, HE HAS BEEN REPAYING THEM WITH THE MOST VALUABLE THING THERE IS: DOG LOVE. RECENTLY, HIS PERFECT SENSE OF SMELL LED HIM RIGHT TO THE ENTRANCE OF A HOSPITAL THAT WAS MORE THAN TWO MILES AWAY FROM HIS HOME. WHY DID HE GO THERE? LET'S LISTEN TO HIS STORY!

Zander: My master, John Dolan, was staying at the hospital. You surely understand that I, as a loyal dog, couldn't let him down, alone and without support.

But how did you manage to track your master?

The Dolans (Zander's masters): Our dog had never been to the hospital; he didn't know the way. He just followed his nose and heart. He didn't care that he had to cross a wide river and a busy intersection. He made it.

Zander: I was upset at first ... I hung around the flat, curled up on John's bed, sometimes howled ... But then I thought: this isn't helping. I have to act! It was quite simple. I simply drew in his scent and followed it all the way to the hospital. Dogs like me have up to 300 million olfactory cells, whereas humans have only 5 million.

Did you go to the hospital on your own?
Yes, exactly. In the middle of the night, so that I didn't wake up my dear master, Mrs. Priscilla, I sneaked out of the house quietly. I passed through busy places, but I didn't give up. The trail ended right in front of the hospital.

And there, one of the doctors helped you, right?
Yes, exactly. They called the phone number on my dog tag. Guess who answered the phone!

Mrs. Priscilla?
No, John. Imagine that! That was really funny. They said: "Sir, your dog is here, please come and pick him up at the hospital." John responded: "But I can't. I'm in the hospital too!" Hah, hah, woof, woof, woof! (Zander is rolling on the floor laughing, ed.)

KARELIAN BEAR DOG ➡️

You may be wondering why I'm called a bear dog. That's simple—like the Russian Laika, I was brought up to hunt bears even under freezing Siberian conditions. Believe me, the bears that spotted me didn't just tremble with cold, ha, ha! I'm brave, have a great sense of smell, and am highly valued by hunters. In addition to bears, I hunt mostly deer and wild boar, which I track by myself, quietly and unnoticed.

⬅️ NORWEGIAN LUNDEHUND

What I'm about to tell you is true. Believe me. Are you ready? Unlike other dogs, I have six fingers! I can also bend my head backwards along my own spine and actually close my ears to keep water out of them ... You wouldn't have believed it of me, would you? Woof! My ancestors used these abilities to hunt puffins on steep sea cliffs. Like them, I'm a brave and resilient dog that can withstand a year-long stay outdoors.

NORDIC GUARD DOGS AND SHEEPDOGS

Don't resist and line up nicely so we can count you. Our instinct tells us to chase reindeer, sheep, poultry, and family members. We are independent and persistent. Mom, dad, son, and the newly born baby ... Phew, we're all here. We can go!

LAPINKOIRA

FINISH LAPPHOUND (LAPINKOIRA) AND LAPPONIAN HERDER (LAPINPOROKOIRA)

We have the blood of shepherd and sheep dogs flowing in our veins. We used to help our masters with herding and guarding reindeer. Nowadays, we do several dog sports. We like to play fetch and we would do anything for our family. We get along with almost everyone, whether they have six, four, or two legs. Even a beginner can train us, but combing our hair and getting rid of thistles takes an experienced hairdresser.

LAPINPOROKOIRA

← NORWEGIAN BUHUND

I'm a dog hero. When you teach me, I will save human lives, help the deaf as an assistance dog, or sniff out hiding places full of drugs . . . You needn't be afraid of anything when you're with me; I'll always protect you. Woof! Just don't ask me to do a somersault—I'll only do it when I want to, woof woof!

SWEDISH VALLHUND ➡

If you're a couch potato, I'll get you to stand up in no time! Do you see the cat behind the fence? The sun is shining beautifully today! Did you say it was raining cats and dogs? It doesn't matter, at least we get to see a rainbow! My great mood is contagious. So don't resist and let's do some sports. I love agility! It's a dog sport with obstacles, I'll teach you. Or let's herd some sheep, one, two, three. In the evening, we can cuddle for a moment, and tomorrow, we will go out again! Wake up!

DOGS' POST

DAILY

392nd YEAR — VOLUME 11 • No. 4696 • TUESDAY, NOVEMBER 23, 2004 • 35 DOG HAIRS

LOYAL HACHIKŌ

Stories of genuine friendship

At Shibuya Station in Tokyo, Japan, there is a beautiful statue of the legendary dog Hachikō, a golden-brown Akita Inu. People had the memorial erected at this site because they wanted to be constantly reminded of great love and incredible dog devotion.

Hachikō was the beloved dog of Hidesaburō Ueno, a Japanese professor at Tokyo University. Every day, the dog walked his master to Shibuya Station and waited for him at the very same spot every night.

On May 21, 1925, no one arrived. One train arrived after another, but Hidesaburō Ueno didn't get off any of them. He couldn't as he had suddenly died that day.

Sad Hachikō was taken in by the deceased professor's relatives. They took care of him with the same love, but Hachikō was still in mourning. He ran to Shibuya Station every day and waited for Hidesaburō just like before. He regularly checked the spot for the long ten years . . . What if his master arrives by chance? Today, his loyalty is commemorated by a bronze memorial embodying true dog love.

MARI AND HER THREE PUPPIES

An interview with puppies

The Dachshund Primary School

WHAT KIND OF LOVE IS THE STRONGEST IN THE WORLD? WE ASKED PUPPIES FROM THE DACHSHUND PRIMARY SCHOOL, AND THE ANSWERS WERE VERY CLEAR—THE TRUEST AND STRONGEST LOVE IS THE ONE BETWEEN A MOTHER AND HER PUPPY. THEN THEY TOLD US A STORY OF MARI AND HER THREE PUPPIES.

Ziggy: Mari was a female Shiba Inu dog that lived in Japan, in the village of Yamakoshi, I think. In 2004, shortly after she gave birth to three healthy puppies, the village was struck by a terrible earthquake. That happens a lot in Japan ...

Andy: They say Mari saved the old man who was taking care of her—she got help for him. Rescuers evacuated him to the neighboring village, and Mari stayed with her kids in the ruined house on her own.

Keira: When Mari ate all the food supplies left by the old man, she and her puppies were really struggling. They were all alone and hungry. Mari had no choice

but to desperately try to look for food. Whenever she found something to eat, she brought it to her puppies, while she was starving.

Bunny: After some time, the old man and his family returned to their home village, sad about losing their beloved Mari. The joy of seeing the four dogs running out from the ruins of the house to greet them was endless. Mari and the puppies easily managed to survive the adversity without human intervention.

Rex: Well, it wasn't that easy. The puppies were cheerful and plump, whereas their mom Mari was a bag of bones because she gave everything to her offspring. And that's what maternal love is all about, right, Mrs. Editor?

What do you think, dear readers? Are the puppies from Dachshund Town right?

SPITZ

Would you like to cuddle with us? Our dense and soft coat is only waiting for you to do it. But we'll see, we'll see: wecan be stubborn, so be patient. We will protect our family until our last breath. After all, our ancestors were wolves. Woof! Woof!

JAPANESE, GERMAN, FINNISH, AND NORDIC SPITZ

We are a fun mixture: originally shepherds, guardian dogs, and bird hunters as well. We are happy to bark it out to you by the family hearth. We are friendly and cuddly toward our humans. We get along well with pets. We love lots of company! So, when are we going to the pet store to bring in another friend?

INTELLIGENCE: 🐾🐾🐾🐾🐾

OBEDIENCE: 🐾🐾🐾

ACTIVITY: Energetic balls (Let's go for a run, shall we?)

GUARDING: 🐾🐾🐾🐾🐾🐾

BARKING: We like barking. Don't you like it too?

FAMILY TYPE: We will protect you like our most precious bone!

IDEAL HOME: If we have enough movement and contact with the owner, we can adapt to living in a flat.

NORDIC SPITZ

FINNISH SPITZ

JAPANESE SPITZ

GERMAN SPITZ

DOGS' POST

Daily

300th YEAR — VOLUME 5 🐾 No. 3586 🐾 THURSDAY, MAY 16, 1912 🐾 35 DOG HAIRS

LADY, WHO SURVIVED THE TITANIC

"Help, we've hit an iceberg! We're sinking!" You might have heard something like this in April 1912, on that unfortunate night, when the icy waters of the North Atlantic forever swallowed the unsinkable ship with the majestic name of the Titanic. It was not only human screams, but also terrified dog barking. Dogs' Post Daily now provides the exclusive testimony of one of the survivors.

"My name is Lady. I am a Pomeranian and I was traveling with my mistress, Miss Margaret Hays. To bark honest, I don't clearly recall what and how it happened back then. After dinner, I was sleeping, when all of a sudden, Margaret woke me up, threw a blanket over me, and ran with me on to the deck.

As she was holding me in her arms, the world swung, and when I finally dared to stick my head out, we were sitting in an inflatable lifeboat on the open sea. I'm telling you, it was truly awful. I've heard a story of a Great Dane who was literally kicked off a lifeboat because it was so huge and took up a lot of space. Woof, woof . . . But enough with such mournful memories. The sun is out, and so am I!"

AMERICAN AKITA

AKITA INU

ASIAN SPITZ AND RELATED BREEDS

We have a more calm and balanced nature than our smaller relatives. But our coat is as thick and cuddly as theirs (we personally measured it with our paws when we met)! We are bigger and sometimes lazy . . . but that doesn't keep us away from barking. Woof!

AKITA INU AND AMERICAN AKITA ⬆

Woof woof! When you hear us bark, it's worth leaving the warmth of your bed. Something must have happened. We are quick to learn new commands, but whether or how fast we can perform them is another thing. We can be willful and stubborn, so be patient with us—it pays off. We are extremely loving and faithful.

CHOW CHOW ➡

No, I didn't drink ink! And even if I did, I wouldn't brag about it; I've got my pride. With my thick coat, I'm the "lion" member of the Spitz family. I come from the Far East, where I helped my masters with hunting and shepherding as a guard or draft dog. I'm a solitary dog, a loner. If you want my trust, you need to earn it!

DOGS' POST

DAILY

323rd YEAR — VOLUME 2 ❦ No. 3859 ❦ SUNDAY, FEBRUARY 10, 1935 ❦ 35 DOG HAIRS

SIGMUND FREUD

JOFI, EXPERT ON HUMAN SOULS

Stories of genuine friendship

When your master is a famous psychologist and therapist, you will receive a great portion of the spotlight as well just because you belong to him, even if you—let's be honest here—do not deserve it. But Chow-Chow Jofi is a whole other story.

Jofi belonged to the renowned psychologist and neurologist Sigmund Freud, who lived in Austria at the turn of the twentieth century. The smart Chow-Chow demonstrated her great talent very soon—she could easily sense the mood of Freud's patients.

"Sigmund was glad when I stayed with him in his office; I helped him a lot. When a patient was fine, I would lie quietly beside him. But when I sensed that the patient was stressed, I got up and stood at the opposite end of the room. Sigmund selected the method of therapy based on that," Jofi recalled.

The popular psychologist loved his dog so much that he even listened to every wish of his little dog expert on human misery. When it was time to go to sleep, Jofi yawned loudly, and big Sigmund ran to bed.

PRIMITIVE DOGS

No, we're not fools, why would you think that? On the contrary, we are among the smartest dogs in the world! We're called "primitive" because our roots go back as far as five thousand years. Try to imagine how ancient we are. Listen carefully to our barking and long howl ... We definitely have something to tell you.

INTELLIGENCE: 🐾🐾🐾🐾🐾🐾
OBEDIENCE: 🐾🐾🐾🐾
ACTIVITY: Hunters
(We need a lot of movement, preferably one that will satisfy our hunting instinct.)
GUARDING: 🐾🐾🐾🐾🐾
BARKING: We bark when we sense danger or prey.
FAMILY TYPE: We believe in "loyalty above all else."
IDEAL HOME: We will live anywhere with our family, even in a flat.

PERUVIAN HAIRLESS DOG

MEXICAN HAIRLESS DOG

← MEXICAN HAIRLESS DOG AND PERUVIAN HAIRLESS DOG

The ancient Inca tribes in Peru and Mexico worshiped us because we were a gift from the gods. Um, and they also sacrificed us to the gods. We were often buried with our owners to keep an eye on them after death. Even today, we can be absolutely devoted to our owner. But please take care of our bare, sensitive skin-protect it from the sun in the summer and give us a warm coat in the winter, pretty please ...

BASENJI →

I come from Congo and I'm the only type of dog in the world that can not bark. You don't believe me, do you? I'll show you now! Compared to others, I can only give out a wide range of much more interesting sounds: I can laugh, whine, hiss and even yodel! In addition, I'm neat and tidy, don't give off a smell, and am a very friendly, tender, and affectionate companion, very fixed to my owner.

OTHERS OF THE SPITZ BREED

1. KOREAN JINDO: I'm a treasure, literally. In 1962, the government of South Korea, where I come from, listed me as a cultural treasure.

2. EURASIER: I'm balanced and sensitive. I'm not at all interested in dogfights.

3. SHIKOKU: You don't know where the north is? Over there! Take me to the other side of the world and I will find my way back due to my great sense of direction.

4. HOKKAIDO KEN: My ancestors from the Japanese island of Hokkaido were athletic and excelled in deer and bear hunting. And I inherited it from them.

5. KISHU INU: I come from Japan, where I helped hunt wild boars and deer 700 years ago. It is even claimed that my forefathers were wolves. Now I know where I got my courage from!

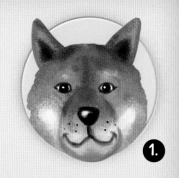
1.

3.

5.

2.

4.

← SHIBA INU

Sit down, lie down, I know very well what you want from me ... but it will be me who decides when to do it. Get used to it, I'm stubborn. In return, my goofy grimace will make you laugh-see? Even now, it looks like I'm smiling at you. We're going to have a lot of fun together because I'm very curious ... But if you need rest, let me sit me near a window for a while; the world will keep me busy.

CANAAN DOG ➡

I know my way in the desert even without a compass. My ancient ancestors lived with the Bedouins in the Negev desert in Israel, helping them guard flocks of sheep. During World War II, people trained me to search for mines. Nowadays, I can also be trained as a guide dog for the blind. I'm intelligent, faithful, and quick to learn. My motto is: help and protect.

PRIMITIVE TYPES— HUNTING DOGS

⬅ THAI RIDGEBACK

I'm almost like a secret agent as, until recently, nobody knew about me outside Thailand. According to ancient writing, my ancestors served as hunters, guards, and travel guides. Look at my back. There's a strip formed by the hair growing in the opposite direction to the rest of the coat! It's called a ridge. Don't worry, the hair doesn't bristle out of fear, it just grows like that. And I'm very proud of it! And by the way, I like to cuddle.

IBIZIAN HOUND ➡

I can elegantly sniff out every rabbit or other small game all by myself, without the help of a hunter. I'm very playful, but you better keep me on a lead. I only get along well with other animals if they don't move. You see, I have a sense of humor! In fact, I prefer the dark one ... Ha, ha, woof woof!

DACHSHUNDS

Welcome among us dachshunds. At first glance, it's clear that we belong among the smaller breeds. Short legs, a long body, and a wise expression on our faces—that's who we are! If we were to say three words that characterize us, it would be: intelligence, stubbornness, and a strong personality. Sure, sometimes we get offended, sometimes we do things our own way, but in the end, we are incredibly loving and sensitive creatures willing to lay down our little dog lives for you. Woof.

INTELLIGENCE: 🐾🐾🐾

OBEDIENCE: 🐾🐾🐾

ACTIVITY: Little adventurers (We enjoy 2 walks per day.)

GUARDING: 🐾🐾🐾🐾

BARKING: What can we say? Our barking is stronger than us . . .

FAMILY TYPE: We are good family pets but often bark at unfamiliar people or animals.

IDEAL HOME: We don't mind a flat.

WIREHAIRED DACHSHUND

Brave, cunning, always with a bit of mischief in our snout-that's us, wirehaired dachshunds. If you want our coat to be well maintained, you have to pluck it from time to time. No, don't laugh, we're not geese! Although we're hunters, we also want to look nice, just like every proper dachshund does. And just like all dachshunds, we are long. Very long. However, our long backbone doesn't do well with long stairs. Take us on the escalators instead!

SMOOTH AND LONGHAIRED DACHSHUND

We are proud to be the oldest types of dachshunds, so our characteristics are the most dachshund-like. Back then, we were much sharper and louder than nowadays, but you know, time and evolution have their impact. What is the advantage of short, smooth hair? You won't get angry at finding tufts of our hair everywhere you look in your flat. On the other hand, in the winter, we get colder than our elegant longhaired friends.

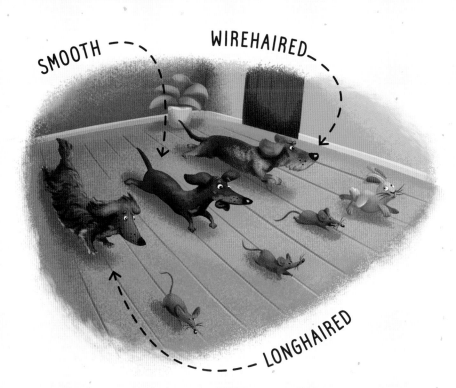

SMOOTH

WIREHAIRED

LONGHAIRED

DOGS' POST

Daily

402nd YEAR — VOLUME 10 🐾 No. 4815 🐾 FRIDAY, OCTOBER 3, 2014 🐾 35 DOG HAIRS

HARLOW, SAGE, AND INDIANA: GREAT LITTLE FRIENDS

Stories of genuine friendship

Dear readers of Dogs' Post Daily, not only is a dog man's best friend, but dogs are also loyal friends to each other, regardless of the breed. Can you imagine a friendship between a huge Weimaraner and a miniature dachshund? You can't? Weimaraner Harlow's story may change your mind.

"Our miniature dachshund Sage has always been my best friend. Actually, she wasn't just my friend, she was more like my sister—loving, loyal, cheerful, and friendly. We had great laughs together. Sage used to ride on my back, and I loved to nudge her with my paw for it. Of course, I was careful not to harm the mite!

Every Christmas, we wished for a nice dog toy and some munchies. And our wishes always came true. We unwrapped our packages, ate, and watched a film with Meryl Streep.

Unfortunately, dachshunds cannot live forever, and Sage went to dog heaven one day. At first, I thought that I would be sad forever. But my masters gave me a new friend, dachshund Indiana. It took some time for me to get used to her, but she won me over with her dark humor. Sometimes, I think she was sent by Sage herself so that I didn't miss her so much. Indiana is my Sage No. 2!"

NAPOLEON, HEROIC BULLDOG

A MONTH AGO, DOGS' POST DAILY ANNOUNCED A CCOMPETITION: WE'RE LOOKING FOR THE BRAVEST DOG OF THE YEAR. WE RECEIVED PLENTY OF STORIES FROM WHICH THE EDITORS PICKED ONE WINNER AFTER CAREFUL CONSIDERATION—THE ONE-YEAR-OLD WHITE ENGLISH BULLDOG, APTLY NAMED NAPOLEON. WHAT DID HE ACHIEVE? HE RISKED HIS OWN LIFE TO PULL A SACK FULL OF DROWNING KITTENS OUT OF THE WATER. THE WHOLE STORY IS TOLD IN THE FOLLOWING INTERVIEW.

  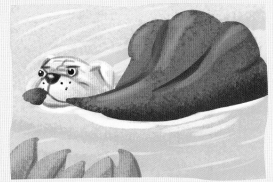

Napoleon, could you recall the day when you became a true hero?
It was a normal day like any other. After lunch, I went for a walk with my master as usual. Suddenly, I heard strange meowing and moaning from the side of the lake. I thought the whole thing was suspicious, so I ran toward the sound. Anyone else would have done the same.

And what did your master do?
He was whistling, calling me back ... You know, otherwise I'm an obedient and well-behaved dog, who responds to all commands immediately. But in that moment, I just couldn't obey. Smothing drove me to the lake, regardless of my master.

That something was a sack with six small kittens.
Yes, I jumped into the water, brrr. I didn't care it was icy, which I don't like, and swam toward the sack like crazy. Phew, even my master realized that there was something wrong and ran to the bank to help me pull the kittens out of the water. We managed to save four of them.

You see, thanks to your intervention, this story has a happy ending. Did you get any reward at home for this heroic act?
You bet! I love a decent steak, so my beloved master bought such a huge portion that I ate it for the next three days. Woof!

Thank you for the interview. We believe that your heroic act will inspire many other dogs.

PINCHERS, SCHNAUZERS, MOLOSSER BREEDS, AND SWISS MOUNTAIN DOGS

We're a fun mixture. Some of us are small, energetic, and sometimes stubborn pinschers and schnauzers. Molossus is a dog of powerful build that resembles a peaceful giant. And kind-hearted mountain dogs do not distinguish all that much between flocks of sheep and their loved ones. But the most important thing is to stay together. This is what we have in common: loyalty and family love.

MOLOSSER BREEDS

ENGLISH BULLDOG →

Oh boy, I love to lie on a couch! While I once helped pull down a full-grown bull like it was nothing, today I'm more of a peace lover. I need an owner who does not overdo it with sports and would rather take care of my skin folds and claws. I get sick sometimes, but as soon as I get better, my dog love can accomplish all kinds of things.

You may be wondering, "wow, what kind of colossus is that?" We're mighty, courageous, and confident creatures with a strong protective instinct developed throughout our long history. We're proud of our majestic muscular figure, and if we lovingly lick you from your chin to your eyebrows, you better get yourself a towel or take some time to dry.

INTELLIGENCE: 🐾🐾🐾🐾🐾

OBEDIENCE: 🐾🐾🐾🐾🐾

ACTIVITY: Occasional athletes (Healthy body, healthy spirit!)

GUARDING: 🐾🐾🐾🐾🐾🐾

BARKING: A good guard is a silent guard. If we bark, there's a reason for it.

FAMILY TYPE: We protect our family to our dying breath.

IDEAL HOME: A house with a garden and the warmth of home will keep us happy.

BULLMASTIFF

ENGLISH MASTIFF

←← ENGLISH MASTIFF AND BULLMASTIFF

I, an English mastiff, am a peaceful giant with a gentle soul, even though I used to be a war dog just like the bullmastiff—who, by the way, is pretty stubborn. He needs an owner who has good experience with dog training. What makes us happy are long walks and right after that, a full bowl of good-quality food. One more bowl, please! Between you and me: did you know that the Mongolian ruler Kublai Khan owned 5,000 mastiffs in the thirteenth century, making him the owner of the largest dog pack ever owned by one man?

NEAPOLITAN MASTIFF →→

I look like a big dog grouch: with my folds and deep wrinkles in my skin, I'm constantly mistaken for being older than I really am. I have to admit that here and there, I really am stubborn and temperamental. I need an owner whom I will respect and can look up to. In return, I will offer them my devotion and loving company. Before you get me, please remember that it is difficult, extremely difficult, for me to be alone.

←← SHAR PEI

Slow down, don't rush me. I'm a quite calm and lazy dog; I have to contemplate everything first. But when I make a decision, I will stubbornly stand by it. I don't really get along well with young children; they love to pull my tail all the time, and I don't like that. But I'm always friendly to my master. My skin—and I have enough for two dogs—feels like sandpaper to the touch. Please do not forget to take care of the folds.

OTHER MOLOSSER BREEDS

1. DOGUE DE BORDEAUX: In ancient times, you could see me on the battlefields standing by my master. I remain loyal and courageous to this day.

2. BROHOLMER: I used to be the favorite of one of the Danish kings. I have tremendous strength but a very gentle and peaceful nature.

3. CANARY MASTIFF: You wouldn't want to hear my deep and intimidating barking in a dark alley.

4. CA DE BOU: I used to fight in a death arena with bulls and bears.

5. TIBETAN MASTIFF: I'm majestic and kind. I come from Tibet, where I protected cattle, villages, and Buddhist temples as a guardian.

GERMAN BOXER ➡

My mom used to say, "A tired boxer is a happy boxer." And she was right. Long walks, that's what makes me happy. Especially when I can return to a warm home, even to a flat. I love children as well. I can play with them indoors and outdoors for hours.

DOGS' POST

DAILY

408th YEAR — VOLUME 1 🐾 No. 4878 🐾 SATURDAY, JANUARY 4, 2020 🐾 35 DOG HAIRS

WHO WAS PERITAS?

WITH YOUR PAW ON YOUR HEART, DO YOU KNOW OUR DOG HISTORY, LEGENDS, AND HEROES? EDITOR DAISY LUCKY INVESTIGATED WHAT THE YOUNGEST PUPPY GENERATION KNOWS ABOUT TIMES PAST IN THE PRIMARY SCHOOL ON MONGREL STREET. OUR DOG PAPER BRINGS A REPORT ENTITLED: WHO WAS PERITAS?

Student Bella: Peritas? Peritas was a huge mastiff that belonged to Alexander the Great, the most famous ancient commander and conqueror.

Student Fluffy: They say that it was Peritas who saved his master Alexander when he and his troops were encircled by the enemy army of the Persian King Darius III. Allegedly, Peritas fought his way through the army and even brought down a dangerous war elephant!

Student Rocky: My mom read to me at home that Alexander the Great got Peritas as a gift from his uncle, the King of Epirus. Peritas was a little puppy back then, and Alexander put him through rigorous training so that he wouldn't be afraid of lions, elephants, or anyone else.

Student Rita: Alexander the Great is said to have loved Peritas very much. He even slept with him in the same bed. Grr, woof. And when Peritas died in battle, he named a city in India after him.

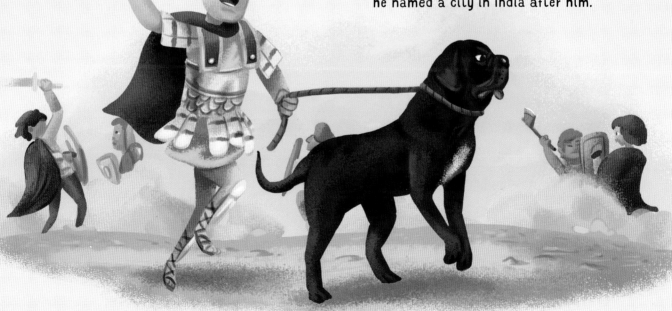

TOSA INU ➦

Quiet and no biting—that was my fighting tactic in "dog sumo" back in Japan. I've stayed courageous and tough to this day, so I will protect you even from falling leaves. Otherwise, I'm a kind and curious companion. I really enjoy long walks and running in wild areas. I bet you can't catch me!

← ST. BERNARD

Over the course of our existence, we have saved dozens of human lives. With our massive paws, we would dig up people trapped by an avalanche in the mountains and transport the wounded to safety. But that's all in the past ... We're still, however, the kind, good-natured giants who have almost a maternal relationship with all people and children. We cannot endure quarrels, screams, swear words, or tension in our family.

NEWFOUNDLAND ➦

Once I'm near water, plop! And I'm swimming. I was originally bred and used as a working dog for fishermen. I like to pull people out of the water, whether they want it or not, just in case they need to be saved. I love humans and other creatures. I'm gentle around children. I can be raised by a less experienced owner, but they should pay special attention to brushing my thick hair regularly.

CANE CORSO ➡

I stood by the side of people in times of great battles in ancient Rome. Even today, I'm a great protector. The longer it takes me—and it does take me a while—to establish a really deep relationship with my owner, the more I'll show then my love. I will be especially appreciative for regular inspections of my sensitive dog ears.

← ROTTWEILER

When I was a puppy, my great-grandfather told me he used to hunt bears. Today, they cannot praise me enough! I work with the police or the army because there is no task in the world that I cannot cope with. But don't worry, you don't have to wear military camouflage to be my master. Let's run together or get on a bike, and see for yourself how I can keep up with you! And I will protect you from any danger with every piece of my body.

GREAT DANE AND DOGO ARGENTINO ➡

I don't mean to brag, but I have a really sweet character: calm, friendly, attentive . . . Training me is not difficult; just occasionally pat me on the back, loudly praise me, and give me a handful of dog treats. My colleague from Argentina, in contrast, acts before she thinks. She used to hunt jaguars, cougars and wild boars for her masters, so it's not surprising that when it comes to her training, being firm is a must. We do have in common our love for the family, to which we devote our dog soul.

GREAT DANE

DOGO ARGENTINO

DOGS' POST

DAILY

379th YEAR — VOLUME 12 ❧ No. 4541 ❧ WEDNESDAY, DECEMBER 14, 1991 ❧ 35 DOG HAIRS

ROTTWEILER EVE: IT WAS BY A HAIR'S BREADTH!

Tales of brave rescuers

Rottweiler Eve demonstrated her courage by pulling her master, Kathie Vaughan, from a burning car at the last minute. And when we say "last minute," we really mean at the last minute. Just see for yourself!

Kathie was confined to a wheelchair and could not go anywhere without it, let alone run. Were it not for quick--witted Eve and her strong teeth, which she used to grip Kathie's ankle and pull her to safety, Kathie would have remained trapped in a car full of black smoke and toxic gases.

When they were both outside, they knew they hadn't made it yet. They had to get away from the car, which could have exploded at any moment. But clever Eve didn't hesitate; she bent down and literally pushed her collar into Kathie's hand. Kathie grabbed it, and Eve pulled her selflessly a few metres away. Just as they reached the spot, there was a deafening bang, and the car exploded. "It was really by a hair's breadth, or maybe two!" they both say today.

JUST NUISANCE

A Window into History

Have you ever heard that we, dog males and females, could become legitimate members of a real human army? It's true, as proved by Just Nuisance, a Great Dane who was officially enlisted in the Royal Navy on August 25, 1939. Dogs' Post Daily presents the recollections of one of the sailors who took care of Just Nuisance:

"Yeah, yeah, Just Nuisance was an absolutely perfect dog, a huge Great Dane. When he stood on his hind legs and leaned against your shoulders, he was intimidating.

When he became one of us, he was given a real tailor-made sailor's hat. He looked great, I tell you. He wore it proudly for every muster or parade. The way he strutted in it ... We couldn't hold a candle to him!

Well, as Just Nuisance became a sailor, he could travel with us by train when we wanted to go out in the evenings. As members of the Royal Navy, we traveled for free. When Just Nuisance was still an ordinary dog, the conductors would get mad at him, sayin' he's a fare dodger, and kicked him out of the carriage; the headquarters even had to pay a fine for him! But when he became a sailor, there was no problem at all. If Just Nuisance hadn't experienced ill health later on, he could have joined the officer ranks. That's how great he was. Credit where credit's due."

DOGS' POST

DAILY

255th YEAR — VOLUME 9 ❀ No. 3050 ❀ FRIDAY, SEPTEMBER 13, 1867 ❀ 35 DOG HAIRS

BARRY, THE ST. BERNARD MOUNTAIN RESCUER

TEENAGE ST. BERNARDS CONSIDER THE PROFESSION OF MOUNTAIN RESCUER TO BE ONE OF THE MOST PRESTIGIOUS JOBS THERE IS. SO DACHSHUNDS, RETRIEVERS, PITBULLS, TERRIERS AND OTHERS, SHOULDN'T BE SURPRISED. THE DESIRE TO HELP IN THE MOUNTAINS FLOWS IN THE VEINS OF EVERY ST. BERNARD. THE STORY OF THE MOST FAMOUS MOUNTAIN RESCUER, BARRY, WILL HELP YOU UNDERSTAND.

St. Bernard Barry
Active duty period: 1800–1812
Place of duty: Great St. Bernard Pass on the Italian-Swiss border.
Employer: the monks of the Great St. Bernard Hospice
Number of people saved: 40

St. Bernard Barry went down in history as the rescuer of pilgrims who were traveling across the Great St. Bernard Pass to Rome. He was supposed to run along the snow--covered paths and guide all the travelers in the right direction. When someone unfortunate got lost and ended up stuck in deep snowdrifts, Barry's job was to sniff and dig them out. They say that he also carried a vessel with fresh warm milk as a welcome first aid for all strays. Once, he even saved a little boy who lost his way and fell asleep in the middle of a dark and cold cave!

NEWFOUNDLAND BARNEY'S REFLECTIONS ON A NAMELESS NEWFOUNDLAND

We, Newfoundland dogs, love water. We don't have webbed feet for nothing—they help us swim better in waves. We are happy to save people and animals that get lost in this unfamiliar aquatic environment and are in danger of drowning. We jump enthusiastically into the water, swim toward them, splash around, grab them by their swimwear and pull them out of the water.

But wait! A majestic Newfoundland on a small fishing boat suddenly jumps into the water, swims toward the drowning man, and patiently waits for the sailors on the ship to pull the man to the safety of the deck. This story actually happened. Do you know, my dear doggies, who my Newfoundland ancestor saved back in the nineteenth century? The Emperor Napoleon Bonaparte! And I am truly proud of this breed, which has webbed paws and loves water and good deeds.

But imagine a raging sea, my friends. One wave rolls over another, the wind is blowing, howling, and gusting, and there is a ship being tossed in the middle of this mess. "Man overboard!" cries its terrified human crew. They can see a man floundering in the water. He is waving his hands, drowning and slowly but surely saying goodbye to his life.

Water sports are great!

Barney

PYRENEAN MOUNTAIN DOG

Woof woof! I like to bark, even at night. I hope you'll forgive me once in a while. Every Pyrenean sheep will confirm that I'm not lacking in courage and protective instinct. I watch all my sheep like the apple of my eye. I guarded the quiet sleep of the Louvre during the reign of Louis XVI. I'm used to acting independently, but I need consistent and patient training.

LEONBERGER

A long time ago, the rulers of all Europe would walk by my side. That's not surprising since I gave them the feeling that they were accompanied by the animal king himself, the lion. The rulers were really impressed by my thick mane, as well as the hairdressers who had to take care of it. But don't be intimidated, I'm not vicious at all—I'm more of a nice lion, I mean a dog, naturally.

LEONBERGER

PYRENEAN MOUNTAIN DOG

SWISS MOUNTAIN DOGS

We're a proud mountain dog breed originating in the Swiss Alps. Our ancestors would spend the whole day in the fresh mountain air, thanks to which we have great strength and a balanced, peaceful character. Above all, we can be immensely gentle toward children and keep an eye on them so that they don't get lost, just like Hansel and Gretel did in that well-known fairy-tale.

INTELLIGENCE: 🐾🐾🐾🐾🐾🐾
OBEDIENCE: 🐾🐾🐾🐾🐾
ACTIVITY: Hard workers (We need to keep our legs and head busy.)
GUARDING: 🐾🐾🐾🐾
BARKING: We are no yappers.
FAMILY TYPE: We wouldn't trade our family for all the dog treats in the world.
IDEAL HOME: House with a big garden, we would love that!

→ BERNESE MOUNTAIN DOG

BERNESE MOUNTAIN DOG AND GREATER SWISS MOUNTAIN DOG

To this day, you can spot us in Switzerland pulling a cart of milk in the mountains. We were originally draft and shepherd dogs. That's why we need plenty of space and long walks livened up by various tasks and antics or chases. Living in an flat in the middle of the city—no, that's not for us!

GREATER SWISS MOUNTAIN DOG

DOGS' POST

DAiLY

401st YEAR — VOLUME 5 🐾 No. 4798 🐾 TUESDAY, MAY 7, 2013 🐾 35 DOG HAIRS

THE BRAVE BRAVE BERNESE MOUNTAIN DOG BELLA

DEAR READERS, WE RECEIVED MANY INTERESTING LETTERS WITH YOUR FUNNY AND THRILLING STORIES THIS MONTH. WE DECIDED TO PRINT THE ONE THAT STIRRED OUR LOYAL AND FAITHFUL DOG HEARTS THE MOST. IT WAS WRITTEN BY A HUMAN READER, CHRIS, TO THANK HIS LOYAL BERNESE MOUNTAIN DOG, BELLA, FOR SAVING HIS LIFE.

"It happened seven years ago. I was at home checking on my lunch in the oven. I injured my ankle in a car accident before, and I fell, holding the hot lunch in a cloth, and hit my head. On the way down, the cloth caught fire from the oven, quickly moving up my arm.

Dear editors, Bella saved my life! Although my house was reduced to ashes, I still have the most important thing in my life: my kind and incredibly brave friend Bella.

Somehow, I managed to remove my shirt and threw it against the wall, but then, the walls of the kitchen caught fire too. It was a nightmare!

I couldn't rise on my own because of my injury and my house was on FIRE! I thought I was doomed when suddenly, I felt something nudging my leg. It was Bella! She licked me with her pink tongue, and I calmed down a bit. She pulled me outside through the only possible escape route until we both stood at a safe distance from the house and could breathe some fresh air."

PiNSCHERS & SCHNAUZERS

Sniff, sniff . . . Did I just smell a mouse passing by? Rodents, watch out! You better hide in holes from us, we're nimble and always ready! We, pinschers and schnauzers, know very well that you people would love to have us as cute and cuddly pets, but oh well—we still have the hunting instinct, so you might have to accept that we need to let it out from time to time.

INTELLIGENCE: 🐾🐾🐾🐾🐾🐾
OBEDIENCE: 🐾🐾🐾
ACTIVITY: Messy (We love being all dirty from mud after a nice chase.)
GUARDING: 🐾🐾🐾🐾🐾🐾
BARKING: We bark, whether we have a reason or not.
FAMILY TYPE: We're happy to join our owners in a bed.
IDEAL HOME: We prefer a house with a garden, but some of us can adapt to living in a flat.

DOBERMANN

Sneak in silently, sniff, and then jump! Vrrr, woof woof! What commotion! I'm a dog that needs to be active all the time! And I also like various tasks, so I don't get bored. That's why I like to serve with the police or army, where I can do my thing: when there is a task, I dive right in, no matter how dangerous it might be. Tension and action, that's what makes me happy! I'm sharp and fearless—I will bare my teeth to all thieves and intruders, vrrr! If my master shows me that they are a natural leaders I will respect them and then, they can introduce me to a family with children.

MiNiATURE PiNSCHER

I might be able to fit in your pocket, but I'm not saying so because I want to hide there. I don't get scared easily—I'm naturally confident! Although I love running, I can adapt to the calmer character of my owner. I like to run next to a bike, and I will accompany you on a mountain hike, but if you occasionally offer to carry me in a bag, you know I won't refuse!

← HOVAWART

Woof woof! I'm an eternal puppy . . . I grow up quite slowly. Fortunately, I'm a calm and loving dog by nature. For my family, I would risk my life, and I need to be in daily contact with you. My owner should be kind to me, but strict.

SCHNAUZERS

In the days of stagecoaches on the roads of Central Europe, we ran alongside horses and slept with the coachman at night. We had a very important task: we protected them and their supplies from intrusive rats. You won't get bored with us. We have a sense of humor, we love movement, and we're quick to learn new commands—those we want to! We can fit into your flat, but we do not mind being in the garden all year long. Brush our coat once a week, and we will be happy. ↓

MEDIUM PEPPER AND SALT

SMALL WHITE

LARGE BLACK

OTHER PiNCHERS, SCHNAUZERS, AND MOLLOSIANS

1. MONKEY TERRIER: I look like a little devil and will always be ready to protect you with my own life. Deal?

2. DUTCH SMOUSHOND: Calm and cool, that's what they call me. Give me a family, and I will love it faithfully for the rest of my life.

3. PINSCHER HARLEQUIN: I'm lively and fast and love being around children. But I'm one of the rare breeds—I'm something like the last dog treat in your pocket!

4. AUSTRIAN SHORT-HAIRED PINSCHER: When there were no fences around Austrian farms, we, Pinschers, were protecting them. Surely you won't be surprised at how much we like to bark. Woof! Woof!

5. GERMAN PINSCHER: Back in the day, you could find me on every farm. Nowadays, I would rather play outside, which I never refuse. Are you sad? I just thought of a great game that will cheer you up!

6. ATLAS SHEPHERD DOG: My ancestors come from the Sahara, where they would be guarding the property of the nomadic Bedouins from wild beasts. That takes courage, doesn't it?

7. BRAZILIAN MASTIFF (FILA BRASILEIRO): I'm known for my self-confidence, stubbornness, and devotion. It's not a coincidence that in Brazil, there's a saying: "faithful as a Fila."

8. BLACK RUSSIAN TERRIER: A lot of owners are amazed at my intelligence and my ability to quickly learn new, stunning tricks.

COMPANION DOGS

You will never be bored with us! We are always fun, and we've been walking side by side with our humans for centuries. In the morning, we wake up the kids by licking their faces, and then we go for a walk with the grandparents. We always have a trick or two up our sleeve to make your day better. Our playfulness and joy are truly contagious. Just wait and see!

INTELLIGENCE: 🐾🐾🐾🐾🐾
OBEDIENCE: 🐾🐾🐾🐾
ACTIVITY: Cuddle buddies (We don't mind being lazy.)
GUARDING: 🐾🐾
BARKING: Woof! What are you doing? Can we help? (We are barking for attention.)
FAMILY TYPE: Kids, adults, grandmas, grandpas ... we love everyone!
IDEAL HOME: Cozy flat, woof!

BiCHONS AND RELATED BREEDS

BiCHON ➡️

A long time ago, during cold nights, I used to warm up the numb legs of noblemen and noblewomen. My fur is so soft that a child has mistaken me for a toy more than once. Haha, woof! I may have a playful nature, but I am no toy! To be honest, I'm not one for sitting around ... I'm a great athlete, and when I see water, splash! I'm swimming. But don't worry, in the evening, I will cuddle with you whether you are noble or not.

⬅️ HAVANESE

Woof woof! I can be a little bit crazy. I like to play, and I'm game for anything, woof! I like kids the best. There are not all that many of us, Havanese, from the island of Cuba; we are rare and literally priceless. With us, you are never going to feel blue—we are born clowns. We are also bright and curious, and we only feel down when we are left alone.

MALTESE

COTON DE TULÉAR

BOLOGNESE

← MALTESE, BOLOGNESE, AND COTON DE TULÉAR

Before you can blink, we will have you wrapped around our finger. We love cuddling, playing, or going on walks with you, whether you are young or old. But don't shout at us, please—that might scare us. If you're angry, just pet our snow-white fur and see how quickly you will calm down. A Coton de Tuléar can walk on its back legs while telling you stories about Madagascar, where they come from. The Maltese loves to play with kids since antiquity, and even the famous philosopher Aristotle mentions it. And the Bolognese is great for people with allergies.

LITTLE LION DOG ➡

I have long, wavy, and silk-like fur that kind of looks like a lion's mane. Rooaaar! Woof! In the sixteenth century, I was a favorite among rich aristocrats. I mean, who wouldn't want to have a lion and a dog in one, right? They even had paintings of me done. You won't come across me all that often on the street these days as I'm quite a rare breed. I'm joyful, affectionate, and playful, and there is no feeling down with me around.

POODLES

MEDIUM

STANDARD

MINIATURE

TOY

← STANDARD, MEDIUM, MINIATURE, AND TOY POODLES

Oh, look at those haircuts! They must be stuck-up, don't you think? That couldn't be further from the truth, hah! Our elegance and noble manners might win us first prizes at dog shows, but we are never too proud to sweat while running or doing other dog sports. After all, we used to be eager duck hunters! Thanks to our balanced and friendly nature, we can be good assistance dogs and are a great choice even for beginners.

CONTINENTAL TOY SPANIELS, RUSSIAN TOY, AND PRAGUE RATTER

PAPILLON AND PHALÈNE →

We may look alike, but at a closer look, you will notice our ears are different—Papillon, which means "butterfly" in French, has erect ears, just like butterfly wings, while I, Phalène, have drooping ears. Our intelligence and playfulness make us great dog athletes. We love agility or dog dancing. Have you heard about dog dancing before? That's when you and your owner do some fun tricks to the rhythm of music. And we have one more unique characteristic—we can sense your mood and immediately make the sadness go away with our playfulness and affection!

PHALÈNE

PAPILLON

← RUSSIAN TOY

Are you thinking about carrying me around in a purse or backpack? I can assure you, that's not the best idea ... all it takes is one side glance, and whoosh, I jump out and I'm gone! Despite my small appearance, I like jumping over obstacles and running next to you on a bike. I am in no way a lazy dog that only likes to lie on the couch all day. Even a beginner can handle my training, and I don't mind living even in the tiniest flat in the whole word. Woof!

PRAGUE RATTER →

I heard a joke that if a ratter sneezes, he will fall on his back ... Very funny, woof! Actually, I'll have you know that I can stand up to any wind gust. Even if it tried to blow me away, I would proudly and loudly stand my ground! Rawr! I used to hunt rats in medieval houses, and that's where my name comes from. I am a chatty dog, who barks about everything around! In addition, I win people over with my loyal, playful, and loving nature, which I'd love to share with you.

BELGIAN DOGS
BELGIAN GRIFFON, BRUSSELS GRIFFON, AND PETIT BRABANÇON

Oh, what's that? Ugh, another cat. We are curious, fearless, and happy dogs, and our keen eyes see everything. We are also very smart, and we all share one thing—we don't need a lead. We're bound to our owners by loyalty and love, and we don't need a rope to prove that because we won't let you out of our sight. We're the ones doing the training here! You can also look forward to our loving snoring at night ...

BELGIAN GRIFFON

BRUSSELS GRIFFON

PETIT BRABANÇON

DOGS' POST

DAILY

405th YEAR — VOLUME 12 🐾 No. 4853 🐾 SUNDAY, DECEMBER 24, 2017 🐾 35 DOG HAIRS

THE BRAVE CHIHUAHUA ZOEY VS. A DANGEROUS RATTLESNAKE

The "Dog Heroines" SERIES

Small is beautiful, people like to say and get themselves cute little Chihuahuas. In all honesty, these gorgeous doggies almost look like toys, and human youngsters just love to cuddle and play with them. But can you believe that such a tiny Chihuahua can also be incredibly brave? Just like Miss Zoey, who saved a toddler from a poisonous rattlesnake.

"We were lucky only because I had decided to take my afternoon nap in the garden and not in my bed," says Zoey who is tiny even for a Chihuahua. "I could hear a weird hiss and something rattling. Something like hisss, rrrrattle . . . And that silent, strange sound was growing closer. I jumped up to see what it was and spotted an enormous rattlesnake. It was making its way right for the baby, who was innocently playing on the grass!"

Zoey started whining, but no one paid any attention to her. In the end, she bravely decided to face the snake herself. "I was trying to chase away that terrible snake with growling and barking, but I was bitten twice. My prospects seemed rather bleak, but I held on until I finally got rid of that dangerous rattlesnake!" says with relief this tiny being with the heart of a lion.

MY FRIEND JUNIOR

Readers' Letters

Dear Dogs' Post Daily,

I am an eager reader of yours and I always look forward to the new issue. I like the stories of brave dog heroes the most. Today, I would like to share one such story with you too.

My friend Junior is a Shih Tzu and he is truly a hero. He once saved seven people at once. Everyone was peacefully asleep when Junior suddenly woke up, smelling smoke. The house was on fire.

Junior started barking and running up and down the last few safe spaces in the house until every single resident woke up and escaped. Trust me, it was right on time! If they had been there even a little bit longer, nobody would have survived.

Dear Dogs' Post Daily, Junior is an incredibly modest dog and does not feel like he did anything extraordinary. But I know he did!

I wish you all the best and good luck!

HAIRLESS DOGS

← CHINESE CRESTED DOG

Do you want to know the recipe for happiness? When you pet my soft and warm skin, all your sorrows disappear. I like to play, learn new things and am very smart . . . sometimes a little crazy, like when I make a race track out of the flat! I'll take off with kicking the cabinet with my hind legs, run under the table, and jump onto the windowsill from the ground, whoosh! And one more time! Did you know that among my brothers and sisters in a litter, at least one puppy will have hair? They're called the Powderpuff, and they warm the other puppies of the litter.

TIBETAN BREEDS

TIBETAN TERRIER

SHIH TZU

LHASA APSO

TIBETAN SPANIEL

CHIHUAHUA

LONGHAIRED AND SHORTHAIRED CHIHUAHUA

Jumping down from the bed can be a challenge for our frail bodies, but coddling us or carrying us around in a bag isn't ideal either. The fact that we are the smallest breed in the world (reaching only about eight inches in height) doesn't stop us from conquering the world under the giant's feet! Hey, you! Go away! Don't get too close to our owners; we can get a bit jealous.

SHORTHAIRED   LONGHAIRED

ENGLISH TOY SPANIELS

CAVALIER, THAT'S ME

CAVALIER KING CHARLES SPANIEL AND KING CHARLES SPANIEL

We inherited our names from the English kings Charles I and Charles II. The say that Charles II loved us very dearly. Supposedly, he spent more time cuddling with us than ruling! The Cavalier was around first, and in the eighteenth century, after the fashion of small round heads and short muzzles, the King Charles breed was born. Our calm, lovable, and friendly nature is admired by many because we are very loyal companions.

LHASA APSO, SHIH TZU, TIBETAN SPANIEL, AND TIBETAN TERRIER

Ding! Can you hear the prayer chimes? Then you're guessing right—our mother-land has Tibetan temples and monasteries. We used to spin the monk's prayer wheels and sit as watchdogs on the walls of temples. The locals considered us sacred and called us bringers of luck (and we didn't say otherwise). We are cuddly, happy, and active by nature. Shih Tzus can run for miles, and they say that people used to build them their own palaces! The Tibetan Spaniel, by contrast, practically behaves like a cat. But beware, even if we look like stuffed toys, we need firm supervision, or we'll take the upper hand. Oh, and don't forget to brush our teeth regularly: we tend to get cavities.

DOGS' POST DAILY

238th YEAR — VOLUME 8 ❧ No. 2845 ❧ SATURDAY, AUGUST 24, 1850 ❧ 35 DOG HAIRS

RICHARD WAGNER IN THE MEMORIES OF HIS DOG, PEPS

Celebrities and Their Dogs

My master, the celebrated composer Richard Wagner, loved animals, especially dogs. He had several dogs throughout his life, but when I look back, I think I was his most significant four-legged love.

I used to sleep in a special basket next to his bed and wake up the well-known musician every morning. All I had to do was gently caress his cheek with my paw. You know,

my master was a great artist and, sometimes, under all the pressure arising from his success and genius, he was a little ... Well, pompous.

Once, I nudged him with my paw when he was reading an important review of his piece ... My master snapped at me at first for disturbing the magnificent Wagner, asking how I dared to do so, and then started laughing at himself—loudly and from the bottom of his heart. Yeah, Richard Wagner.

I even had a bark when it came to his work. Every time he composed something new, he put me in the chair next to the piano and started playing. When I didn't like something or some part didn't seem right to me, I barked, and Richard Wagner changed the passage.

Yes, I'm glad that I could meet and love the great Wagner. He was truly outstanding, and I did my best to prevent him from growing too arrogant and absorbed by his fame so as not to damage our special relationship.

~ Peps, Cavalier King Charles Spaniel ~

PEKINGESE AND JAPANESE CHIN

JAPANESE CHIN ➡

I'm a little bit like a cat: kind, sensitive, and friendly to people and animals alike. I have enough confidence to admit that I can even learn to use the cat box. And like a cat, I seek out high spaces from where I can observe my surroundings, and I'm also quiet and lick my paws ... Cats just know where it's at, meow! Oh, sorry, woof!

SMALL MOLOSSIAN DOGS

BOSTON TERRIER

PUG

FRENCH BULLDOG

⬅ PEKINGESE

Shh, don't tell anyone! I'll let you in on a secret: when nobody's watching, I like to lie on freshly washed bed sheets. Lounging on soft pillows, mmm! I'm not really that active, and when I do decide to get up from my bed, I waddle around calmly and slowly. I was worshipped as a sacred dog during the Tang dynasty in the eighth century! And if someone stole me, they could be executed for it. So, aristocracy is in my blood, and people even say that I am stubborn and haughty ... but you know how it is, woof!

PUG, BOSTON TERRIER, AND FRENCH BULLDOG

We have been loyal companions for centuries, and we do it with grace, regardless of the snoring or farting of the Bulldog and the French Terrier ... We are playful and sometimes, a bit stubborn. We can look grumpy, but there's more than meets the eye. Most of the time, we are joyful little dogs that only need your companionship for happiness. When we do something naughty, please don't punish us with harsh words—we tend to take them too much to heart.

DOGS' POST DAILY

403rd YEAR — VOLUME 4 ❖ No. 4821 ❖ WEDNESDAY, APRIL 8, 2015 ❖ 35 DOG HAIRS

EVERYONE CAN WEAR A SMILE!

IF YOU EVER MEET A CHEERFUL DOG WITH A BUNCH OF CHEERFUL KIDS AND THEY HAVE SOMETHING IN COMMON—THAT IS, A SMALLER OR A BIGGER SCAR ABOVE THEIR UPPER LIPS, YOU JUST MET A DOG WITH A HUGE HEART—LENTIL, THE FRENCH BULLDOG.

Lentil, could you tell us more about your story?
Well, I was born in 2013 with a bilateral cleft palate. The breeder gave me away and I'm only still here in this world thanks to my new mistress Lindsay. She took me under her wing and fed me with a special tube every two hours during my first few months of life.

Lindsay: We needed Lentil to get stronger so that he could undergo palate surgery.

And what came next?
Lentil: Next came a successful operation and a brilliant idea. You know, I'm not the only one born with this singularity. It turned out there were a lot of children with a cleft palate and, unlike us dogs, it bothers them. They feel unattractive, though for no reason.

Lindsay: Long story short, we came up with an idea to bring Lentil together with kids with the same scar above their lips. You can't imagine their reactions—their faces and souls brightened up instantly knowing they weren't alone. Lentil is truly helping them accept themselves the way they are and feel comfortable in their bodies.

Without a doubt, you're a true hero with your heart in the right place, Lentil.
Lentil: Oh, c'mon! Me, a hero? More like my dear human friends are because they're not afraid anymore to smile regardless of the size of their scars.

~ For Dogs' Post Daily: Barking Baguette ~

SERGEANT STUBBY

The "Dog Heroes" SERIES

FOR BOYS, GIRLS, MOMS, AND DADS IN CAMO SUITS—SIMPLY FOR ALL LOVERS OF MILITARY HISTORY—DOG PAPERS BRINGS YOU AN INTERVIEW WITH HISTORIAN POODLE FREDDY ON THE HISTORICAL SIGNIFICANCE OF THE BOSTON TERRIER SERGEANT STUBBY IN THE FIRST WORLD WAR.

Mr. Freddy, who was Sergeant Stubby?

Stubby was a Boston Terrier that belonged to the US-enlisted private Conroy. During the First World War, Conroy sneaked his little friend to Europe as support in fierce battles.

And was he supportive?

He was more than that! It turned out that Stubby was not only a cute companion but also a great fighter. In short, he saved a soldier's life more than once.

Mr. Freddy, could you be more specific?

Stubby had great hearing—he could hear shellfire from several miles away and warn the troops in time. He did it in his own special way. He rested his head on the ground, stuck his bottom out, and the human fighters quickly made their way to safety. His smell was, of course, much more sensitive than that of his companions, so he could warn people against dangerous war gases.

Mr. Freddy, was it common for a dog to receive a military rank in the human world?

No, sir, it wasn't common at all. Stubby was the first U.S. Army dog ever to be promoted to the officer rank. His exquisite military coat shone with a number of military awards, which was also rare and extraordinary.

MARIE ANTOINETTE'S PUG

Doggie princess
and princesses

A fairy-tale page
for puppies

In times gone by, there lived a Pug from an ancient lineage of Pugs. How cheerful and playful he was! The princess who received him as a gift fell in love with him immediately. The princess' name was Marie Antoinette. When she was a little girl, she could play with her beloved Pug all she wanted. They would run together in the gardens, jump up and down, and play tug-of-war with the princess' silk ribbons. But the time came for Marie to marry. Her mother sent her in a carriage to France, where her groom—Louis XVI of France awaited her. At the French border, she had to change from her Austrian clothes into a French crinoline skirt and, in fact, put aside everything Austrian . . . even her beloved Pug. Oh come on, don't growl at her, pups, it wasn't her fault. Just like you, she also had to obey every command. But don't you worry, the princess never forgot her dog. Actually, as soon as she could, she begged for her Pug to be brought to her. At the court, the Pug met lots of local puppies and grown-up dogs, and Marie Antoinette would pamper them all during their long walks in the royal gardens.

The dog lady who rode the longest wave: a Kelpie named Abbie Girl holds the record for the longest wave sufred by a dog: a 350-ft-long wave in open water.

DOG RECORD HOLDERS

🐾 **Skillful jumper:** an English greyhound lady named Feather—as in, light as a feather—jumped over a 75-inch-high obstacle.

🐾 **World's heaviest dog:** the English Mastiff Zorba weighed in at 343 lbs.

🐾 **World's smallest dog:** Chihuahua Milly measured only a little over 3,8 in.

🐾 **World's tallest dog:** Zeus, the Great Dane, when standing on his hind legs, reached a height of 7 ft 4 in.

🐾 **Dog lady with the longest tongue:** a boxer dog named Brandy had a 17-in-long tongue. Incredible!

Enthusiastic skateboarder: Otto the Skateboarding Bulldog (French Bulldog) slid through the legs of 30 people on a skateboard.

HOW TO TAKE CARE OF DOGS

🐾 Feed us twice a day with a measured portion of dry and juicy food and give us fresh water. Please do not give us chocolate, nuts, or onions—we can't eat those like you, people.

🐾 Walk us every day and let us run. We can have a great time together, especially in a dog training area! You should keep us on a lead and put on a protective muzzle when we are in public.

🐾 Play with us regularly and teach us the basic commands: come, stay, or fetch. Do not punish us when we make a mistake when training. Instead, reward us for good behavior with, for example, a dog treat, yummy! Basically, let us know that you love us.

🐾 At least once a year, take us to a vet who can get us rid of worms and vaccinate us so we don't get sick.

🐾 Brush our teeth every day or buy us dried buffalo skin or chewing sticks.

🐾 Regularly cut our claws and brush our hair. We can put up with a thorough bath around once a month!

🐾 Prepare a comfortable bed for us, which will be ours.

🐾 Introduce us to all family members, including other pets.

WHEN A DOG GETS LOST, THE LABEL ON ITS COLLAR WILL HELP!

COLLAR LABEL

Do you want to do a good deed? If you're thinking about getting a dog with your parents, go to the local shelter. There are a lot of dogs and puppies waiting for a real home. You will definitely fall in love with one!

A DICTIONARY OF DOG SPEECH

Based on our body posture and behavior, you can easily tell how we feel or what we want to tell you:

1. Lying on our back with our belly exposed: "I trust you."

2. Relaxed posture, joyful wagging tail: "Let's be friends!"

3. Crouching and shaky posture with lowered ears, tail tucked between legs: "I'm afraid."

4. Paws stretched forward, rear up in the air, tongue out: "Let's play!"

5. Wide stance, aggressive growling and barking: "I'm furious!"

E. Dobiášová, Š. Sekaninová & J. Sedláčková

ATLAS OF DOGS

Illustrations by Marcel Králik

© Designed by B4U Publishing for Albatros,
an imprint of Albatros Media Group, 2021.
5. května 22, Prague 4, Czech Republic
Printed in China by Leo Paper Group.

ISBN: 978-80-00-05935-8